The Holographic Mind

Exploring the Intersection of Neuroscience and Virtual Reality

Oliver Cook

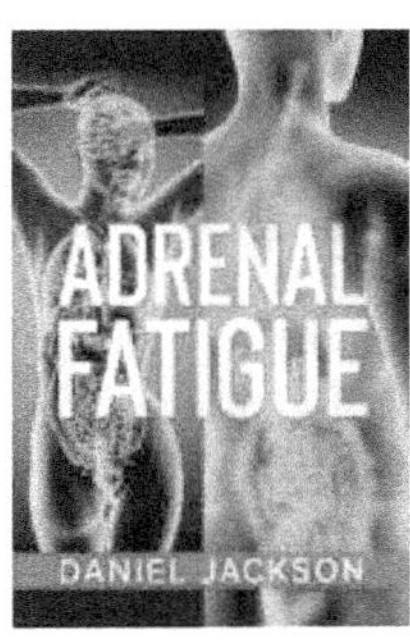

Take a look at more great books available from Rockwood Publishing

... some for FREE!

Just visit the link below:

rockwoodpublishing.co.uk

Contents

Introduction

Welcome to a journey into the very essence of perception, reality, and self. A path that will lead us down the rabbit hole of the mind and the digital universe.

The core premise of our exploration?

A theory that has the potential to revolutionize not only how we understand the human mind, but how we interact with our world. This is the holographic mind hypothesis.

What if I told you that the same principles that allow a hologram to project a three-dimensional image from a two-dimensional surface could be applied to the way our brain processes, stores, and recalls information? It might sound far-fetched, yet it is a scientific hypothesis that is gaining momentum.

The holographic mind hypothesis suggests our brains are essentially holographic systems, encoding and decoding vast amounts of information in a way that creates our rich, multifaceted perception of reality.

Setting the Stage: Unpacking the Holographic Mind Hypothesis

Before we delve deeper, let's take a moment to understand what we mean by 'holographic'. A hologram is a physical structure that diffracts light into an image. The unique aspect of a hologram is that every part of the hologram contains all the information possessed by the whole. The 'whole in every part' nature of a hologram provides us with a new way of understanding organization and order.

Imagine the holographic mind like a vast, intricate network. Each node in this network contains not just its own individual data, but a complete map of the entire network. This could explain how our minds are capable of such incredible feats of memory, recall, and association.

A Glimpse at the Holographic Universe

The holographic principle, a cornerstone of string theories and a radical new view of the universe, suggests that the entire universe can be seen as a two-dimensional information structure "painted" on the cosmological horizon, such that the three dimensions we observe are merely an effective description at low energies.

Physicist David Bohm, one of the proponents of the theory, suggests that the universe itself may be "holographic," i.e., even reality could be a kind of giant, cosmic-scale hologram. A startling idea, isn't it? But let's remember - all models are wrong, but some are useful. The holographic principle, whether ultimately accurate or not, provides us with a new, useful way to understand the nature of reality and the fundamental structure of the cosmos.

The Brain: A Holographic Storage Network?

How does our brain, a three-pound organ, store so much information, and retrieve it with such precision? The answer might lie in the holographic theory of mind. Like a hologram, the brain may contain memory and sensory impressions in a 'distributed' manner. Instead of specific 'locations' in the brain for memories, impressions, or skills, each part of the brain may contain fragments of information that can be fully reconstructed with the whole.

This model of brain function aligns with what we observe in brain imaging studies and in cases of brain injury where localized damage does not obliterate specific memories or capabilities. Neuroplasticity, the brain's ability to reorganize and heal itself, also makes more sense in the context of a holographic brain. After all, if information isn't stored in one place but distributed across the whole, the system is more resilient and adaptable.

The Conscious Experience: A Holographic Projection?

But what about our conscious experience? If our brains operate holographically, what does this say about our subjective experiences of reality?

Think about a virtual reality headset. When we wear one, we're fully immersed in a three-dimensional experience. Yet all that information is coming from a two-dimensional screen inches from our eyes. The headset doesn't change reality; it alters our perception of it. In a similar way, the holographic mind hypothesis suggests our brains may create our rich, complex perception of the world from information stored in a seemingly "distributed" way.

When you recall a memory, you often don't just remember facts. You remember sights, sounds, smells, emotions - a full, three-dimensional sensory and emotional experience. This 'holographic' recall is akin to your brain pulling up a fully immersive 'virtual reality' experience from a seemingly two-dimensional storage network.

Further still, consider the phenomenon of dreams. In our dream states, we experience worlds, narratives, sensations, and emotions that are entirely constructed by the mind. Here, our brain becomes not just a holographic storage network but also a holographic projector, creating rich, immersive experiences entirely from within.

However, don't confuse this with suggesting that our reality is a mere illusion or a simulation. The holographic mind hypothesis is a model, a metaphor that helps us understand the mind's vast capabilities. It's about understanding how our mind encodes, processes, and recalls information in a way that produces our complex perception of reality.

In essence, the holographic mind hypothesis paints a picture of the brain as an amazing computational device, capable of creating immersive, multifaceted experiences of reality. It's a theory that challenges our traditional understanding of consciousness and opens up new possibilities for understanding the mind and the nature of reality. Welcome to the journey into the holographic mind.

Reality Engine: Virtual Reality and its Impact on Human Perception

Virtual Reality (VR), as a concept, has captured the human imagination for decades. The notion of being able to immerse ourselves fully in a digitally created environment is exciting, almost bordering on the fantastical. Yet, here we are in an era where VR is not just real but increasingly accessible.

In its early days, VR was predominantly linked with gaming. Who wouldn't be thrilled by the idea of stepping into a fantastical world, casting spells or battling intergalactic foes, all from the comfort of your living room? The rush of adrenaline, the feeling of truly being "in" the game rather than just playing it, provided an unparalleled sense of immersion and enjoyment.

From Gaming to Cognitive Science: The Journey of Virtual Reality

But VR's journey did not stop at gaming. Far from it. As the technology advanced, its potential implications for fields outside of entertainment became increasingly clear. The same principles that allow a gamer to explore a digital realm could allow a surgeon to practice a complex operation, a designer to walk through a building not yet built, or a teacher to take their students on a virtual field trip to ancient Rome.

In particular, the intersection of VR with cognitive science has been especially fascinating. By providing a controlled, immersive environment, VR offers a unique opportunity to study human cognition and perception in a way that was not possible before.

Imagine a cognitive scientist trying to understand how we perceive space. With VR, they can alter the virtual environment in subtle ways and study how those changes impact the subject's perception and navigation. This allows us to better understand how our brains construct our sense of spatial awareness and how it adapts to changes.

It's not just spatial perception either. VR has been used to explore everything from memory and attention to the psychology of empathy. For instance, a study might place participants in a virtual environment as a different gender, race, or even species, then measure how this shift in perspective influences their attitudes and behaviors.

Implications of the Holographic Mind Hypothesis

The holographic mind hypothesis provides an interesting lens through which to view the impact of VR on human cognition. If our minds indeed operate holographically, creating rich, three-dimensional experiences from a "distributed" network of information, then VR can be seen as a kind of externalized, digital equivalent of this process. Just as our brains may pull from a network of distributed information to create our perception of reality, VR pulls from a database of digital information to construct an immersive experience. The holographic mind can be seen as the ultimate "reality engine", with VR as a technological mirror of this incredible capability.

Towards the Future

VR's journey, from gaming to cognitive science, is still just beginning. The rise of VR technology presents us with exciting new opportunities for understanding the mind and human perception. It can be an essential tool in cognitive science research, providing new insights into how we perceive and interact with the world around us.

More broadly, the intersection of VR and the holographic mind hypothesis can provide us with a fresh perspective on the nature of reality and consciousness. As we continue to explore this territory, we may find that our digital and cognitive realities are more intertwined than we ever thought possible.

Virtual Embodiment: Blurring the Boundaries between Self and Avatar

Let's take a moment to consider our relationship with our bodies. Our sense of self is so deeply intertwined with our physical form that it's difficult to separate the two. But what happens when we immerse ourselves in a virtual environment and take on a digital body, an avatar? How does this new form, not made of flesh and blood but pixels and polygons, influence our sense of self? This phenomenon, known as 'virtual embodiment', lies at the fascinating intersection of technology, psychology, and neuroscience.

A New Skin: The Avatar as an Extension of Self

When you don a VR headset and step into a virtual world, one of the first things you often do is choose or create an avatar. This digital representation isn't just a puppet. In a very real sense, it becomes an extension of yourself, a conduit for your interactions within the virtual environment.

What's striking is how quickly and deeply we can identify with these virtual bodies. A mere hint of human-like movement in our virtual hands, a reflection in a digital mirror, or the shadow of our avatar on the virtual ground can be enough to trigger a sense of embodiment. Suddenly, the avatar doesn't just represent you - it feels like 'you'.

The Proteus Effect: Changing Ourselves by Changing Our Avatars

What's even more intriguing is how our avatars can influence our perceptions, attitudes, and behaviors - a phenomenon known as the 'Proteus effect'. For instance, if you choose an avatar that's taller than your actual height, you might find yourself behaving more confidently in the virtual world. Conversely, embodying an avatar of the opposite gender can encourage empathy and understanding for different gender experiences.

The Proteus effect isn't confined to the virtual realm either. Studies suggest that our experiences as our avatars can spill over into our real-world behaviors. After a session of embodying a fit, athletic avatar, you might find yourself more motivated to exercise. Spending time as an avatar that's older than you might make you more empathetic towards the elderly.

Through the Lens of the Holographic Mind

Let's circle back to our holographic mind hypothesis. If we view our conscious experience as a kind of holographic projection, the phenomenon of virtual embodiment becomes less surprising.

Consider the fact that our minds are already masters of constructing reality. Every day, we perceive the world around us, process a flood of sensory information, and synthesize it into a coherent, continuous experience. We map our bodies, understand their position in space, their interaction with the world, and project this knowledge into our conscious experience.

In the context of VR, our holographic mind is simply doing what it does best - making sense of a new 'reality'. It accepts the digital input of the VR system and integrates it into our existing perceptual framework. It adapts, re-calibrates, and then projects our consciousness into the new digital 'body'. Our holographic minds, it seems, are more adaptable and flexible than we ever imagined.

Merging Realities: The Future of Virtual Embodiment

As VR technology continues to evolve, the boundaries between our physical selves and our avatars will likely become increasingly blurred. Full body tracking, haptic feedback, even digital smell and taste could deepen our sense of virtual embodiment.

But the implications extend beyond mere technology. As our understanding of the mind and consciousness grows, especially through the lens of theories like the holographic mind, we'll have a richer comprehension of these phenomena.

The realm of virtual embodiment offers an extraordinary opportunity to explore the nature of self and consciousness, to challenge our ideas about identity, and to expand our understanding of empathy and experience.

It's yet another exciting aspect of the intersection of VR and neuroscience, and another area where the holographic mind hypothesis can provide us with valuable insights.

Imagine, for instance, the potential for therapy and personal growth. What if you could embody an avatar that represents a version of yourself you aspire to be, and then bring those traits back into your real-world persona? What about the possibilities for fostering empathy and understanding by experiencing life from different perspectives?

Or consider the implications for identity and self-expression. In the virtual realm, you can be anyone, or anything. You can experiment with different identities, explore aspects of your self that might feel constrained in the real world, and create an avatar that truly reflects your inner self.

The exploration of virtual embodiment could also shed light on deeper philosophical questions. What makes you 'you'? Is identity tied to our physical bodies, or is it something more abstract, more fluid? Can we maintain a continuous sense of self even when our 'bodies' change?

The holographic mind hypothesis suggests that our conscious experience is a kind of 'projection' of information processed by the brain.

With virtual embodiment, we're extending that projection into a new kind of reality, offering a unique opportunity to explore and understand the malleability and resilience of consciousness.

In the end, our exploration of virtual embodiment could lead to a profound shift in how we understand ourselves and interact with each other. It's a shift that could have far-reaching implications, not just for VR and cognitive science, but for society as a whole.

Virtual Worlds, Real Emotions: Understanding the Psychological Impact of VR

When you think about the concept of virtual reality, it's easy to focus on the 'virtual' part. The detailed environments, the avatars, the physics, and interactions. But there's another component to the experience that's equally vital and intriguing - the 'reality' part. How does experiencing these virtual worlds impact our emotions and psychology? And what does this tell us about the human mind?

Feeling Virtually Real

Firstly, it's essential to acknowledge a fundamental truth: the emotions and psychological reactions we experience in VR are genuinely real.

If you've ever gasped in awe at a beautiful virtual sunrise, felt your heart pound as you battled a virtual monster, or felt a pang of sadness during a poignant moment in a VR narrative, you know this firsthand.

In fact, it's this ability to elicit real emotions that gives VR its power. It's what makes VR experiences engaging and immersive. It's what allows us to suspend our disbelief and accept the virtual world as 'real' for the duration of our experience.

But why does VR have this emotional impact? A lot of it has to do with presence - the sense of 'being there' in the virtual environment. Our brains are incredibly good at adapting to new inputs and environments. When you put on a VR headset, your brain quickly begins to accept the virtual sensory input it's receiving, especially if the environment responds to your actions in a realistic way.

The Psychological Impact of VR

Given this emotional resonance, it's no surprise that VR can have a profound psychological impact. For instance, researchers have successfully used VR to treat conditions like post-traumatic stress disorder (PTSD) and phobias. By gradually exposing patients to the things they fear in a controlled, safe virtual environment, therapists can help them overcome their anxieties.

On a lighter note, VR can also induce positive emotional states. Virtual environments that evoke feelings of awe and wonder, for instance, have been shown to boost mood and even promote pro-social behaviors. These experiences can foster a greater sense of connection to others and the world around us, demonstrating VR's potential as a tool for promoting mental well-being.

VR through the Lens of the Holographic Mind

From the perspective of the holographic mind hypothesis, the emotional impact of VR makes perfect sense. If our brains are indeed creating a kind of holographic projection of our conscious experience, then a virtual environment is simply another form of 'input' for that projection.
In other words, our holographic minds don't distinguish between 'real' and 'virtual' in the way we might think. They process the sensory input they receive, whether from the physical world or a virtual one, and integrate it into our conscious experience. If that input triggers an emotional response, we feel it - truly and deeply.

Future Implications

As VR continues to evolve, it's likely that its psychological impact will only grow. As virtual environments become more realistic, more responsive, and more emotionally engaging, our reactions will become even more potent. VR could become a powerful tool for therapy, personal development, education, and more.

At the same time, the intersection of VR and psychology also poses new questions and challenges. How can we ensure that VR is used responsibly and ethically? How do we balance the benefits of VR therapy with potential risks, such as re-traumatization or over-reliance on virtual experiences?

These are complex issues that will require careful thought and research. As we explore them, we'll also deepen our understanding of the mind, consciousness, and the nature of reality. The holographic mind hypothesis and other theories like it will continue to provide valuable insights and guide us on this journey.

Part I: The Basics of the Holographic Mind and Virtual Reality

Understanding the Holographic Principle: From Quantum Physics to Neuroscience

In 1947, a clever British-Hungarian scientist named Dennis Gabor invented the hologram, a three-dimensional image stored in a two-dimensional surface. It was a groundbreaking innovation that completely turned the concept of imaging on its head. Fast-forward to the present day, the holographic principle has expanded far beyond just Gabor's innovation, now stretching its fingers into the realms of quantum physics and neuroscience, amongst other disciplines. But to get there, we need to start at the very beginning. So, let's embark on this captivating journey to understand the holographic principle and its implications.

The Basics of Holography

To get our feet wet, let's start with what we can see and touch - the physical hologram. A hologram, at its core, is a way of storing and reproducing a three-dimensional image in a two-dimensional medium. Unlike a photograph, which captures only the intensity of light, a hologram captures both the intensity and phase of light. It's the phase of the light that carries the information about the depth, hence allowing us to perceive the image in three dimensions.

Now, if you've ever marveled at a holographic sticker, you've experienced the magic of holography. But how does it work?

The creation of a hologram involves the use of a laser beam, which is split into two separate beams: the reference beam and the object beam. The object beam bounces off the object you want to create a hologram of. These two beams then intersect and interfere with each other. The resulting interference pattern is recorded on a photographic plate. Voila, you have a hologram!

Each point on this holographic plate contains the whole image information. So, if you were to cut the plate into pieces, each piece would still be able to reconstruct the whole image, albeit with a lower resolution. This property is unique to holography and forms the essence of the holographic principle.

Now, let's take a leap from the tangible to the abstract. From physical holography to quantum physics and neuroscience. How does the holographic principle find relevance in these fields?

The Holographic Principle: A Quantum Leap

The holographic principle stems from the study of black holes in the field of quantum gravity. It was physicist Leonard Susskind who first suggested that the information contained within a black hole might be entirely encoded on its two-dimensional event horizon - the boundary around a black hole beyond which nothing can escape.

This was a revolutionary idea! Why? Because it suggested that the information in three dimensions could be represented in two dimensions, much like a physical hologram. This idea was extrapolated to the universe as a whole, proposing that our perceived three-dimensional reality might be just a holographic projection of information stored on a distant two-dimensional surface.

The Holographic Mind: A New Paradigm in Neuroscience

Now, what does this have to do with our minds? Quite a bit, as it turns out. If the universe can be described as a hologram, what about the human brain? After all, it's the most complex object in the known universe.

The theory of the "holographic mind" suggests that our minds construct a three-dimensional image of the world from the two-dimensional visual signals we receive. Just like a hologram, this mental image allows us to perceive depth and navigate through space.

The holographic mind theory goes one step further, postulating that memories are stored in the brain in a similar fashion to holograms. The idea is that each part of the brain may contain the whole of the memory, rather than individual memories being localized to specific neurons or groups of neurons. This could explain why damage to one part of the brain doesn't necessarily result in losing specific memories or capabilities but instead can result in more general memory loss or impairment.

Now, let's draw a line to another intriguing field – the realm of virtual reality.

The Intersection of the Holographic Mind and Virtual Reality

It is here, at the intersection of the holographic mind and virtual reality (VR), where things start to get truly exciting. Virtual Reality technology has advanced in leaps and bounds, offering immersive experiences that play tricks on our perception. But how do these two concepts connect?

VR exploits the holographic nature of our mind. It feeds our senses with carefully crafted two-dimensional signals (images and sounds) which our brains then process into a perceived three-dimensional experience. The result? An immersive, seemingly "real" virtual world that we can explore and interact with.

The real charm of VR is its ability to deliver experiences that trick our brains into believing we are somewhere else. You could be sitting in your living room in reality but, through VR, your brain perceives that you're walking on the moon, or diving deep under the sea.

By understanding the nature of the holographic mind, we can create more convincing, immersive virtual realities. Moreover, studying how our minds react to these artificially constructed realities can, in turn, provide more insights into the nature of perception and reality.

Understanding the holographic principle and the basics of holography is the key to unraveling the mysteries of the holographic mind and its connection with virtual reality. It's a journey that takes us through the realms of physics, neuroscience, and digital technology, each one illuminating the others in surprising ways.

We've only scratched the surface here, laying down the basic understanding needed to delve deeper into these intertwined disciplines. As we navigate through the subsequent chapters, we'll explore more about how the mind works, how virtual reality plays its part in our perception of reality, and how these two fields are increasingly influencing each other.

Brace yourself for an exciting voyage into the depths of your mind, the intricate layers of virtual reality, and the blurry boundaries between the two. Welcome aboard the journey to understanding the holographic mind. Buckle up, keep your mind open, and enjoy the ride.

From Quantum Holography to Neuropsychology

Taking a journey from quantum holography to neuropsychology may seem like quite a leap. At first glance, these two fields might appear to be worlds apart. However, once we begin exploring the theoretical frameworks that shape them, we realize that there's an enthralling story connecting the two, a story that is far from obvious but absolutely thrilling in its implications. Let's embark on this intellectual journey and see where it leads us.

Quantum Holography: The Cosmic Code

In our previous discussion, we touched upon the holographic principle in quantum physics - the idea that our three-dimensional reality could be a projection of information stored on a distant two-dimensional surface. But there's more to it when we dig deeper.

One key realization that emerges from quantum holography is the notion that the universe at its most fundamental level might be composed of bits of information, much like a cosmic hologram. The holographic principle in quantum gravity suggests that the maximum amount of information contained in a region of space is proportional to the region's surface area, not its volume. This implies that reality might be fundamentally two-dimensional, with the three-dimensional world as we know it being a kind of holographic projection of this underlying reality.

This principle doesn't just apply to black holes or the universe as a whole. It is also thought to apply to any system described by quantum mechanics, which, in essence, is every physical system in the universe.

A Bridge to the Brain: Holographic Neural Networks

Having established a basic understanding of quantum holography, let's cross over to the realm of neuroscience. How can the holographic principle, conceived in the world of quantum physics, translate to the human brain and our understanding of it?

Enter the field of neuropsychology, the study of the structure and function of the brain as they relate to psychological processes and behaviors. Here, the idea of the brain as a holographic storage system begins to take shape. This theory, known as the holographic brain theory, suggests that our brain uses holographic principles to create a spatially mapped, three-dimensional model of the world and store information.

The human brain, like a hologram, doesn't store information at discrete locations. Instead, information is stored diffusely throughout the brain. This means, akin to a hologram, each part of the brain may contain the entire piece of information, much like how each part of a holographic plate contains the entire image.

This model explains certain enigmatic aspects of brain function. For instance, why can some brain-damaged patients retain near-full mental capacities even after losing significant parts of their brain? The holographic brain model suggests it's because each part of the brain contains a whole yet blurrier version of the perceptual information.

The notion of holography in neural networks also aligns well with the idea of neural plasticity, the brain's ability to reorganize itself by forming new neural connections throughout life. The brain's inherent redundancy, as suggested by the holographic model, allows it to adapt and reconfigure even in the face of injury or damage.

Virtual Reality and Neuropsychology

Understanding our brain's holographic nature can tremendously benefit fields like Virtual Reality. When designing VR experiences, we can leverage this knowledge to create environments that our brain can map and interpret efficiently, leading to more immersive and realistic virtual experiences.

Moreover, Virtual Reality finds its application in neuropsychology as a tool for both research and treatment. VR can create controlled environments to study cognitive processes and behavior, offering valuable insights into our brain's functioning. In the therapeutic context, VR is used in exposure therapy for phobias and PTSD, in cognitive therapy for stroke rehabilitation, and in pain management, to name just a few.

In these therapeutic contexts, understanding the brain's holographic nature is crucial. We know that each part of the brain contains a whole representation of information. Using this knowledge, VR-based therapies can target the brain's plasticity, aiding patients in developing new neural pathways, compensating for the areas that have been damaged or are malfunctioning.

The Future of Quantum Holography and Neuropsychology

So, where does the interplay of quantum holography and neuropsychology lead us? The potential is awe-inspiring. If we continue to unravel the principles of quantum holography and apply them to our understanding of the brain, we could unlock unprecedented avenues in neuroscience and neuropsychology.

One fascinating implication of the holographic principle is the idea that the entirety of the universe is interconnected at a fundamental level. Applying this idea to neuroscience suggests that each part of our brain is inherently interconnected. This holistic view of brain function could revolutionize our understanding of mental processes, potentially leading to breakthroughs in treating neurological disorders and enhancing cognitive function.

On the technology front, this understanding could shape the future of virtual reality and even spawn entirely new fields. Imagine a VR system that could fully engage with our holographic brains, offering experiences that are indistinguishable from real life, or a neuropsychological treatment that can precisely target the brain's holographic storage to cure memory-related diseases.

From quantum holography to neuropsychology, we're beginning to see the world and ourselves in an entirely new light. It's a journey that's as challenging as it is thrilling, pushing the boundaries of our understanding of reality, both the reality of the universe and the reality created by our minds.

So, we find that a concept that arose in quantum physics, grappling with the nature of black holes, finds resonance in understanding the human brain's workings, our perceptions, and our behaviors.

This amazing cross-pollination of ideas is truly the beauty of interdisciplinary exploration. It's a testament to the interconnectedness of knowledge and the boundless potential of human curiosity.

Let's continue to explore and question, to connect the dots between seemingly disparate ideas. Who knows what thrilling revelations the next chapter might hold? After all, every bit of knowledge, every new understanding, is a piece of the vast cosmic hologram we're all part of.

The Holonomic Brain Theory: Karl Pribram and David Bohm's Legacy

Two formidable figures stand as pillars in the realm of the holographic mind and brain theory - neuropsychologist Karl Pribram and quantum physicist David Bohm. Their contributions form the bedrock of the Holonomic Brain Theory, a groundbreaking model that fundamentally reshapes our understanding of the brain and consciousness.

The Groundwork: Karl Pribram's Insights

Karl Pribram, a renowned neuroscientist and psychologist, was among the first to propose that the brain operates according to holographic principles. His work was initially motivated by a simple question: How do we store memories? Traditional theories suggested that specific memories were stored in specific locations in the brain. Yet, there was growing evidence that memory was not localized in this way.

Pribram's curiosity led him down a path of discovery, ultimately culminating in what we now know as the Holonomic Brain Theory. This theory proposes that our brains construct a holographic, spatially mapped image of the world, with memories and information diffusely distributed throughout this brain-generated hologram.

The beauty of Pribram's model is that it can explain some fascinating aspects of memory. For instance, how is it possible that memory doesn't degrade as the brain loses neurons over time? Or how can memories remain intact even after significant parts of the brain are removed or damaged?

According to the holonomic brain theory, just as every part of a hologram contains the whole image, every part of the brain may contain all the information processed by the brain. This non-locality of memory storage in the brain would explain these seemingly perplexing phenomena.

David Bohm: Quantum Physics Meets Consciousness

While Pribram was formulating his ideas, physicist David Bohm was revolutionizing the world of quantum physics. Bohm proposed a radical interpretation of quantum theory known as the "holographic universe" or "implicate order". According to this model, the universe is fundamentally interconnected at a level deeper than the apparent separateness we see in the physical world.

Bohm's interpretation of quantum mechanics suggests that at a deeper level of reality, everything is a single, unbroken, flowing process - the implicate order. The tangible reality we perceive, the "explicate order", is just the surface layer of this deeper realm, much like the three-dimensional image is the surface layer of a holographic plate.

The Intersection: Holonomic Brain Theory

It was the intersection of Pribram's and Bohm's ideas that gave rise to the Holonomic Brain Theory. Pribram realized that Bohm's interpretation of quantum mechanics could provide the underlying physical mechanism for the brain's holographic properties.

In this model, each part of the brain contains the whole of the memory and cognitive information, with individual memories distributed throughout the brain in a holographic manner. This is akin to Bohm's implicate order, where each part contains information about the whole.

The Legacy and Beyond

The Holonomic Brain Theory profoundly influences our understanding of cognition, consciousness, and even the nature of reality itself. It supports a holistic perspective, viewing the brain as an interconnected whole rather than a mere collection of parts.

Moreover, the theory suggests fascinating possibilities for our understanding of consciousness. If our brains operate on holographic principles and our universe might itself be holographic, as Bohm proposed, then consciousness could be a more integral part of the universe's structure than we've previously imagined.

This theory also opens up exciting avenues for technology and therapy. It informs the development of more immersive VR experiences, playing a crucial role in how we design systems that interact with our holographic minds. Therapeutically, it helps us understand why certain cognitive therapies work and how we can enhance them for better outcomes.

Furthermore, the Holonomic Brain Theory sheds light on phenomena that were once considered inexplicable. For instance, the mystery surrounding 'phantom limbs', where amputees continue to experience sensations from a limb that is no longer there. The holographic model of the brain, with its premise of each part containing the whole, may hold the key to understanding such phenomena.

Pribram's and Bohm's legacy in the field of neuropsychology and quantum physics has been immensely influential and continues to guide current research. Scientists today are still exploring the connections between the holographic model of brain function and quantum physics, looking for more definitive evidence to support or challenge the Holonomic Brain Theory.

It is crucial to remember that, as groundbreaking as the Holonomic Brain Theory is, it remains one model among many. The brain is incredibly complex, and our understanding of it continues to evolve. As we uncover more about its structure and function, theories like this one will be honed, expanded, and sometimes overturned.

The Holonomic Brain Theory, born out of the intellectual partnership of Karl Pribram and David Bohm, stands as a testament to the power of interdisciplinary thinking. It draws a line connecting the dots from the inner workings of our brain to the fundamental structure of the universe.

Exploring this theory opens up not just a new understanding of the brain and consciousness but also a new appreciation for the intricate interconnectedness of knowledge across different disciplines. It serves as a potent reminder that the quest for knowledge is a journey without end, where every answer uncovers new questions and every discovery paves the way for more exploration.

As we delve deeper into the holographic mind, let's remember Pribram and Bohm's legacy - their audacity to think differently, their tenacity to explore uncharted territories, and their humility to accept that we are only scratching the surface of understanding the majestic mystery that is the human brain.

May their journey inspire us as we continue our voyage into the mesmerizing world of the holographic mind, uncovering the secrets that lie within, around, and beyond us. As we continue our exploration, we will find ourselves not just learning about the brain and reality but also growing in our capacity to wonder, question, and discover. Here's to the adventure that awaits us in the realm of the holographic mind!

The VR Revolution: Technologies Shaping Our Alternate Realities

The Evolution of Virtual Reality Technology

The world of Virtual Reality (VR) is one of the most exciting landscapes in modern technology. It's a domain where science fiction collides with reality, where our wildest dreams of exploring alternate realities are being realized. But how did we get here? And where are we heading? To answer these questions, we'll need to trace the evolution of VR technology, highlighting the breakthroughs that have shaped this fascinating field.

Humble Beginnings: A Dream of Virtual Worlds

The concept of a simulated reality is far from new. As early as the 1860s, we see evidence of humans trying to create immersive experiences. With panoramic paintings and 360-degree murals, artists strove to transport viewers into different worlds, providing immersive experiences of far-off places or historic events.

The dream of virtual reality, as we understand it today, took a more definitive shape in the 20th century. Science fiction authors, like Stanley G. Weinbaum in his short story "Pygmalion's Spectacles", conceptualized the idea of a device that can mimic all five senses, projecting a comprehensive simulation of reality.

Birth of VR: The Sword of Damocles

The first true VR system, known as "The Sword of Damocles," came into existence in the late 1960s, created by Ivan Sutherland and his student Bob Sproull. The device was named so because of its threatening appearance - a large contraption suspended from the ceiling. It was primitive by today's standards, providing wireframe room and object simulations, but it laid the groundwork for future VR technologies.

The '80s and '90s: A New Wave of Innovation

The 1980s and '90s were exciting times for VR. Jaron Lanier, one of the pioneers in the field, popularized the term "virtual reality" during this period. His company, VPL Research, developed some of the first VR devices, including the DataGlove and the EyePhone head-mounted display.

At the same time, NASA was also exploring VR as a tool for flight simulation and remote control of rovers in space. The Virtual Interface Environment Workstation (VIEW) project led to significant advancements in VR technology and applications.

The 21st Century: The Dawn of Consumer VR

The dream of consumer VR had always been there, but it was in the early 21st century that this dream began to take shape.

The advent of smartphones triggered a revolution in display technology, making small, high-resolution screens both affordable and widely available.

In 2010, Palmer Luckey, a teenager passionate about VR, capitalized on these advances to create the first prototype of the Oculus Rift. This device, while still rudimentary, represented a massive leap forward in the quest for consumer-friendly VR technology. The Oculus Rift caught the attention of Mark Zuckerberg, leading to Facebook acquiring Oculus VR in 2014, which further accelerated the development of VR technology.

Today: The Golden Age of VR

We're now living in what many consider the golden age of VR. Devices like Oculus Quest 2, PlayStation VR, HTC Vive, and others have made high-quality virtual experiences accessible to millions of users worldwide. These headsets provide immersive experiences with high-resolution displays, precise head-tracking, and increasingly intuitive control schemes.

Moreover, we're witnessing an explosion in VR content, from immersive video games and educational apps to virtual meetings and therapeutic tools. These applications are continually pushing the boundaries of VR technology, driving the development of more advanced hardware and software solutions.

The Future: A New Era of Holographic VR

As we look towards the future, we're on the cusp of a new era in VR - holographic VR. Taking inspiration from the holographic principle and advancements in light field technology, the future of VR might not just be about strapping screens to our faces, but rather creating interactive holographic environments that we can see and touch.

Companies like Microsoft with their HoloLens, and Magic Leap with their mixed reality headset, are pioneering the integration of VR with augmented reality (AR). These technologies aim to superimpose holographic images onto our real-world view, blending the digital and physical realms seamlessly.

We're also seeing advancements in haptic feedback technology, which aims to simulate the sense of touch in the virtual world. Gloves with haptic feedback, vests that allow users to feel virtual impacts, and even devices that use ultrasound or electric signals to simulate tactile sensations without direct contact, are on the horizon.

Another fascinating area of research is brain-computer interfaces (BCIs) for VR. The idea here is to bypass traditional control schemes altogether, allowing users to interact with virtual worlds using only their thoughts.

Elon Musk's company, Neuralink, is one of the organizations leading the charge in this field, although we're still years, if not decades, from this technology reaching mainstream adoption.

As we can see, the evolution of VR technology is a testament to human imagination and ingenuity. From the panoramic murals of the 19th century to the cutting-edge holographic VR systems of today, each step has been an adventurous leap towards making our dreams of virtual exploration a reality.

This journey is far from over. As we continue to uncover the secrets of the holographic mind and build ever more advanced VR systems, the line between the physical and virtual will become increasingly blurred. We are indeed standing on the brink of a world where our experiences are only limited by our imagination.

The VR revolution is here, and it's transforming not just how we play games or watch movies, but also how we learn, how we work, how we socialize, and how we perceive reality itself. It's an exciting time to be alive, and we can't wait to see where this journey takes us next.

The Neuroscience of Virtual Reality: How VR Hijacks Our Senses

Virtual reality is a powerful tool that can take our minds on a journey to places we can only dream of, from alien worlds to forgotten epochs, and even into the intricacies of the human body. But how exactly does VR manage to convince our brain that we're somewhere we're not? To understand this, we need to delve into the fascinating field of neuroscience and see how VR plays tricks on our senses and perception.

The Senses: VR's Gateway to the Brain

Our perception of reality is a construct that our brain forms based on the input it receives from our senses - vision, hearing, touch, smell, and taste. VR targets these senses, particularly vision and hearing, with meticulously engineered stimuli that mimic those we would encounter in real environments.

In terms of vision, VR headsets occupy the majority of our visual field, projecting stereoscopic images that create an illusion of depth and distance. This tricks our brain into perceiving a three-dimensional environment, an illusion further reinforced by tracking our head movements and adjusting the visual field accordingly.

For hearing, VR systems use binaural or spatial audio, which simulates the way sounds differ in each ear based on the location of the sound source. This gives a sense of directionality and distance, further immersing us into the virtual world.

Hijacking Perception: Sensory Conflict and Presence

The essence of VR's convincing illusion lies in its ability to create a sense of 'presence' – the feeling of being 'inside' the virtual world. This is achieved by creating a sensory alignment or consistency between various sensory inputs and our actions.

For instance, when you turn your head in a VR environment, the visual scene shifts correspondingly. When you reach out to grab a virtual object, your hand (represented by a controller) moves synchronously. This sensory alignment tricks your brain into accepting the virtual world as your operative reality.

However, this illusion can be shattered when there's a conflict between sensory inputs or between your senses and your expectations. This is why latency – the delay between your action (e.g., turning your head) and the corresponding change in the visual scene – is a critical factor in VR systems. High latency can lead to a breakdown of the illusion of presence and can even cause motion sickness, a common issue in early VR systems.

Going Beyond Sight and Sound: The Frontier of Full Immersion

While current VR systems primarily focus on sight and sound, the ultimate goal is to engage all our senses, creating fully immersive experiences. This means simulating touch (haptics), and possibly even taste and smell.

Haptic technology is already making significant strides. From vibrating controllers that simulate the 'feel' of actions, to more sophisticated gloves that can simulate the texture of virtual objects, we're getting closer to being able to 'touch' the virtual world.

The simulation of taste and smell, however, is still largely in the realm of research. These are complex senses to replicate, as they involve intricate chemical processes. However, some researchers and companies are exploring ways to create smell and taste simulations, opening up the tantalizing possibility of fully multi-sensory VR experiences in the future.

The Neuroscience of VR: Impact on the Brain

VR doesn't just fool our senses – it also impacts our brain in intriguing ways. Studies have shown that navigating a virtual environment can activate the same regions of the brain that are involved in real-world navigation. VR experiences can also evoke strong emotional reactions and have been used therapeutically, for example, to treat phobias or post-traumatic stress disorder.

However, it's important to remember that the neuroscience of VR is still a young field, and there's much we don't know. As VR technology evolves and becomes more pervasive, it is critical to continue studying its effects on our brain and cognition. Questions about how long-term exposure to VR might impact our perception, attention, memory, and even social cognition are still open areas of research.

The Brain-Computer Interfaces: The Future of VR

The future of VR might be even more intertwined with our brains, thanks to the development of brain-computer interfaces (BCIs). These devices translate brain activity into computer commands and can potentially provide a more natural and intuitive way to interact with virtual environments.

For instance, instead of using a controller to pick up a virtual object, you might simply think about the action, and the BCI would translate this intention into the corresponding command. While still in the early stages of development, BCIs for VR could revolutionize how we interact with virtual worlds, making the experiences even more immersive and personal.

Understanding the neuroscience of virtual reality helps us appreciate the complexity and ingenuity of this transformative technology. VR is more than just cool tech; it's a testament to our deep understanding of human perception and our ability to leverage this knowledge to create experiences that captivate our senses and minds.

However, it also raises intriguing questions about the nature of reality, perception, and the mind itself. If our brain can accept a virtual world as real, what does that tell us about the nature of reality and our perception of it? As we delve deeper into the world of VR and uncover its impact on our brain, we might find ourselves not just exploring new realities, but also gaining new insights into the oldest mystery of all - the nature of human consciousness.

As we stand on the precipice of even more advanced VR technologies, the line between the virtual and the real continues to blur. VR offers us the tools to create and explore realities beyond our physical constraints, opening up limitless possibilities for creativity, exploration, and understanding. In the process, we are not just reshaping our perception of reality but also expanding the horizons of the human mind.

Emerging Technologies in VR: Brain-Computer Interfaces and Beyond

As we continue to push the boundaries of virtual reality (VR), the focus is not just on refining the technologies we have but also on exploring entirely new ways of creating and interacting with virtual worlds. The potential applications of these emerging technologies range from entertainment and education to healthcare and beyond. Let's explore some of these promising frontiers, starting with the exciting world of Brain-Computer Interfaces (BCIs).

Brain-Computer Interfaces: Bridging Minds and Machines

Brain-Computer Interfaces are devices that provide direct communication pathways between the brain and an external device, bypassing the need for traditional input methods like keyboards, mice, or VR controllers. BCIs hold enormous potential for VR, promising to make interactions with virtual environments more natural, immersive, and intuitive.

Imagine navigating a virtual world simply by thinking about where you want to go or interacting with virtual objects using thought commands. This might sound like science fiction, but researchers and tech companies worldwide are working on making this a reality.

One of the leaders in this field is Neuralink, a company co-founded by Elon Musk. Neuralink is developing an implantable BCI with the long-term goal of enabling symbiosis between humans and artificial intelligence. While this technology is primarily aimed at helping individuals with neurological conditions, the implications for VR could be profound.

However, developing a practical and safe BCI for VR is fraught with challenges, both technical and ethical. These range from achieving the necessary precision in detecting and interpreting brain signals to addressing concerns about privacy, security, and the long-term effects of interfacing our brains with technology.

Haptics: The Future of Touch in VR

As we've discussed earlier, the sense of touch plays a critical role in our perception of reality, and replicating it in VR is a significant challenge. The field of haptics, which involves creating artificial sensations of touch, is making great strides in this area.

Several companies are developing haptic gloves that can simulate the sensation of touching different objects in VR. These gloves use a variety of technologies, from mechanical systems that physically resist your fingers when you 'touch' a virtual object, to electrical stimulation that tricks your brain into feeling different textures.

At the cutting edge, some researchers are exploring the use of ultrasound or even directed energy to create haptic feedback in mid-air, without the need for gloves or other wearable devices. This technology is still in the early stages, but it could revolutionize how we interact with virtual environments.

Mixed Reality: Blurring the Lines Between Real and Virtual

Mixed reality (MR) is another emerging field with exciting implications for VR. MR systems, like Microsoft's HoloLens, overlay virtual objects onto the real world, creating a hybrid environment where physical and virtual elements coexist and interact in real-time.

By blending the digital and physical realms, MR opens up new possibilities for VR applications. For instance, architects could use MR to visualize and manipulate 3D models of their designs in the context of a real site, or medical students could study 3D, interactive models of the human body superimposed on a study partner.

Emerging technologies in VR, from BCIs to advanced haptics and mixed reality, are not just enhancing the quality of virtual experiences but also fundamentally redefining how we interact with virtual worlds.

These advancements are pushing the boundaries of our imagination and unlocking new applications that we're only starting to envision.

However, with these advancements also come challenges and questions. How can we ensure that these technologies are safe and respect our privacy? How will they impact our brains, our behavior, and our society?

These are important questions that researchers, developers, policymakers, and all of us as a society need to engage with as we move forward.

Part II: Recent Research and Developments

The Holographic Mind Revisited: Recent Discoveries and Perspectives

The holographic principle, which we explored in Part I, posits that all the information in a volume of space can be described on a boundary surface. In the context of the mind, this suggests that our cognitive processes might not be localized in discrete brain areas but distributed in neural networks across the brain, much like a hologram.

This notion of a holographic mind, first proposed by neuroscientist Karl Pribram and physicist David Bohm, continues to be a subject of active research and debate. Recent discoveries in neuroscience and cognitive science provide fascinating perspectives that further elucidate this concept.

For instance, advanced neuroimaging techniques have revealed that our brain is a dynamic, interconnected network, with billions of neurons constantly forming and reforming connections in complex patterns. This aligns with the idea of a holographic mind, where cognitive processes arise from the intricate interplay of neural activity across the brain.

Moreover, researchers have found that different parts of the brain can take over functions typically associated with other regions when needed, a phenomenon known as neuroplasticity. This further supports the idea of a distributed, rather than localized, cognitive processing system.

Recent research in memory consolidation during sleep also points towards a potential holographic aspect of our minds. It seems that memories are not stored in single, specific locations. Instead, they are encoded in unique, distributed patterns of neural activity, further strengthening the holographic hypothesis.

New Insights into Neural Networks: From Neurons to Neural Holography

While the idea of a holographic mind might sound abstract, it becomes more tangible when we delve into the intricate world of neural networks. A neural network, in this context, refers to the interconnected web of neurons in our brains. It's through these networks that information flows, is processed, and ultimately forms our thoughts, memories, and consciousness.

Traditionally, neuroscience has focused on understanding individual neurons - their structure, function, and how they transmit signals. But to truly appreciate the mind's holographic nature, we need to examine the broader picture: how neurons form networks, how these networks interact, and how they give rise to complex cognitive functions.

This field of study, often referred to as connectomics, is becoming increasingly important in neuroscience. By mapping out the connections between neurons - the brain's 'wiring diagram' - researchers hope to uncover the neural network patterns that correspond to different thoughts, feelings, and experiences. This could offer insights into the holographic nature of cognitive processes. Furthermore, advanced imaging techniques like two-photon microscopy are allowing us to visualize neural networks in unprecedented detail. For instance, these techniques can show neurons firing in real-time, illuminating the dynamic nature of neural networks.

There's also growing interest in how quantum mechanics, the branch of physics that deals with phenomena on the tiniest scales, might play a role in neural networks. Some researchers suggest that quantum effects could underlie the brain's computational power, potentially adding a whole new dimension to our understanding of the holographic mind.

While these theories are still in the realm of speculation, they underline the exciting potential of recent developments in neuroscience and related fields. As we delve deeper into the neural networks that underpin our minds, we are bound to uncover new insights that challenge our understanding of cognition and consciousness.

Unraveling the Complexity of Neural Networks

The complexity of neural networks in the brain is staggering. Comprising an estimated 86 billion neurons, each with up to 10,000 connections or synapses with other neurons, these networks form a highly interconnected web of information processing pathways.

Yet, despite their complexity, neural networks are remarkably efficient. They can process vast amounts of information in parallel, adapting and learning from experience. This dynamic, adaptive nature is thought to underlie many aspects of cognition, from perception and memory to decision-making and consciousness.

While the principles of neural network operation are well-established, understanding how they give rise to complex cognitive functions is a considerable challenge. Researchers are tackling this by studying neural networks at various scales.

On the smallest scale, they're looking at how individual neurons transmit and process information. This involves understanding the electrical and chemical processes that drive neuron firing and synaptic transmission. It also involves studying the plasticity of synapses, or how their strength changes with use, a phenomenon thought to underlie learning and memory.

On a larger scale, researchers are studying how neurons form circuits and networks. This involves mapping the 'wiring diagram' of the brain, or connectome, and understanding how information flows through these networks. It also involves studying how different brain regions communicate and coordinate their activity.

Neural Holography: A New Perspective on Neural Networks

As we've seen, neural networks are complex, dynamic, and distributed, much like a hologram. This has led some researchers to propose that our brains might operate on principles similar to those of holography, a concept known as neural holography.

In a hologram, each part contains information about the whole. Similarly, in neural holography, each part of the neural network contains information about the entire network. This could explain how our brains can process information so efficiently and how they can adapt and reorganize in response to damage or new experiences.

This concept also ties in with theories of distributed processing in the brain, where cognitive functions are thought to arise from the coordinated activity of many neurons across the brain, rather than being localized in specific areas.

While still a speculative idea, neural holography has exciting implications. If true, it could offer a new way of understanding how our brains work and how they give rise to our thoughts, feelings, and consciousness. It could also inspire new approaches to artificial intelligence and machine learning, providing a blueprint for creating more efficient and adaptable artificial neural networks.

Quantum Effects in Neural Networks

Finally, as we venture into the realm of the very small, we encounter the world of quantum mechanics. Some researchers speculate that quantum effects might play a role in the brain's neural networks, potentially contributing to their efficiency and computational power.

Quantum mechanics is the branch of physics that deals with phenomena on the smallest scales, such as atoms and subatomic particles. It's known for its strange and counterintuitive principles, such as superposition (the ability of particles to exist in multiple states at once) and entanglement (the ability of particles to instantaneously affect each other, regardless of distance).

While the brain is a warm, wet environment that seems ill-suited for delicate quantum effects, recent research suggests that quantum phenomena might be more robust than previously thought. Some researchers propose that quantum effects could occur in the brain, potentially playing a role in neural communication and information processing.

For instance, it's been suggested that quantum effects could enhance the sensitivity of neurons, allowing them to respond to incredibly small changes in their environment. Others propose that quantum effects could underlie the brain's ability to process information in parallel or to store information in a distributed, holographic manner.

While these ideas are still highly speculative, they highlight the exciting potential of quantum biology, an emerging field that explores the role of quantum mechanics in biological systems. Should these quantum effects prove to be a fundamental part of brain function, it could radically reshape our understanding of neural networks and the concept of the holographic mind.

Brain Imaging Technologies: Unveiling the Neural Hologram

Technological advancements play a critical role in exploring these ambitious concepts and theories. Advanced brain imaging technologies, such as functional Magnetic Resonance Imaging (fMRI), two-photon microscopy, and optogenetics, are providing researchers with an unprecedented view of neural networks in action.

fMRI allows scientists to capture dynamic images of the entire brain at work, illuminating the large-scale networks involved in different cognitive tasks. While its resolution is limited, preventing it from capturing individual neurons, it provides invaluable insights into the brain's overall organization and function.

On the other end of the spectrum, two-photon microscopy and optogenetics allow researchers to visualize and manipulate individual neurons with remarkable precision. They can observe how neurons fire in real-time, track the formation and dissolution of synapses, and even control neuronal activity with light. These techniques are providing a detailed view of the neural network's workings, laying the groundwork for a deeper understanding of the holographic mind.

Artificial Intelligence and Neural Networks: Mirroring the Holographic Mind

Interestingly, developments in the field of artificial intelligence (AI) and machine learning are also contributing to our understanding of neural networks and the holographic mind. Deep learning, a branch of AI, utilizes artificial neural networks inspired by the brain's structure and function.

In particular, the concept of distributed representations in deep learning echoes the holographic mind principle. Rather than storing information in a specific location, deep learning algorithms represent information as patterns of activity distributed across the artificial neural network. This method increases the efficiency and robustness of information processing, much like our brains.

While artificial neural networks are still crude approximations of their biological counterparts, they provide a practical framework for testing theories about the brain. They also open the possibility of creating AI systems with similar efficiency and adaptability to the human brain, potentially leading to breakthroughs in AI and machine learning.

Moving Forward: Challenges and Implications

While these developments are exciting, the path to understanding the brain's holographic nature is fraught with challenges. The sheer complexity of neural networks and the lack of methods to directly observe their operation in real-time represent significant hurdles.

Moreover, theories involving quantum effects in the brain are still highly speculative and far from being accepted by the scientific community. They will require substantial empirical evidence and theoretical support to gain acceptance.

Nonetheless, the concept of the holographic mind, bolstered by developments in neuroscience, AI, and quantum biology, offers a tantalizing perspective on the nature of the brain and consciousness. Should these theories hold, they could have profound implications for neuroscience, psychology, AI, and our understanding of what it means to be human.

Quantum Information Theory: A Bridge between Neuroscience and Holography?

In the quest to understand the interconnection between the mind's operations and the physical world, researchers have long sought a framework that can reconcile the macroscopic world of neuroscience with the microscopic universe of quantum physics. One candidate for this bridge is Quantum Information Theory (QIT), a branch of science that explores the quantum-level characteristics of information and how it can be manipulated.

When applied to neuroscience and holography, QIT offers tantalizing insights, bridging the gap between these seemingly disparate domains. To appreciate the potential of this fascinating intersection, we first need to understand the principles of quantum information and how they contrast with classical information theory.

Information in a Quantum World

In classical information theory, the fundamental unit of information is the bit, which can be in one of two states - usually represented as 0 or 1. In contrast, quantum information is encoded in quantum bits or qubits. Unlike classical bits, qubits can be in a superposition of states, meaning they can exist as 0, 1, or any combination of both.

The superposition principle allows quantum systems to represent and process vast amounts of information simultaneously, potentially giving them enormous computational power. But that's not all. Quantum systems also exhibit entanglement, a phenomenon where particles become linked and instantaneously affect each other's states, regardless of the distance between them. This unique feature can significantly enhance communication and information processing in quantum systems.

Quantum Information Theory Meets Neuroscience

While the idea of quantum processes playing a role in brain function is not new, QIT provides a framework to explore this concept more systematically. The brain, after all, is an information processing system, and understanding the fundamental nature of the information it processes could shed light on its workings.

A key point of interest is whether the brain might exploit the unique features of quantum information - superposition and entanglement - to enhance its computational capabilities. Some researchers have suggested that quantum effects could underlie various neural processes, from the sensitivity of sensory neurons to the coordinated activity of neural networks.

For instance, some studies suggest that quantum effects might play a role in olfaction, the sense of smell. According to this theory, molecules have a particular smell because of the specific way they vibrate, and these vibrations could trigger quantum effects in the olfactory receptors in our noses.

Another intriguing hypothesis involves quantum effects in microtubules, small structures within neurons that help maintain their shape and function. Some researchers propose that these microtubules might act as quantum processors, carrying out complex computations within individual neurons.

While these ideas are still speculative and controversial, they point towards the exciting potential of a quantum perspective on brain function. If proven true, they could revolutionize our understanding of the mind, consciousness, and the nature of reality itself.

Holography and Quantum Information Theory

When it comes to holography, QIT also offers compelling insights. Recall the holographic principle from earlier discussions: information about a volume of space can be fully described on its boundary surface. This principle originates from quantum gravity research and reflects quantum information's key properties.

In a quantum hologram, information is distributed across the system, and each part of the system contains information about the whole. This is reminiscent of the brain's distributed processing, where cognitive functions emerge from patterns of activity across neural networks rather than being localized to specific areas.

This parallel has led some researchers to speculate that the brain might function as a quantum hologram, leveraging the unique properties of quantum information to carry out complex cognitive tasks. This perspective offers a potential explanation for various aspects of brain function that remain poorly understood, such as how memories are stored and retrieved, and how consciousness arises from physical processes.

Bridging the Gap

With these pieces of the puzzle in place, we can now begin to appreciate the bridge that Quantum Information Theory builds between neuroscience and holography. By providing a framework that encapsulates the inherent characteristics of quantum physics—like entanglement and superposition—QIT can potentially help us understand how our neurons, at their most fundamental level, process information.

For instance, if we can prove that neurons or their components, such as microtubules, indeed harness quantum properties, we might just find ourselves with a more comprehensive model of how our brains encode experiences into memory. Or we could gain a better understanding of how our senses can detect and process stimuli at extraordinarily low thresholds—potentially via quantum interactions.

On a larger scale, understanding the brain as a quantum information processor could shed light on its extraordinary efficiency and adaptability. It could explain how the brain can process vast amounts of information in parallel, adapt to new experiences, and reorganize itself in response to damage or learning.

At the same time, interpreting the brain's neural networks as a form of quantum holography might help solve some of the long-standing mysteries of neuroscience. How does the brain integrate information from diverse regions into a unified perceptual experience? How does it generate the subjective experience of consciousness? And how does it store and retrieve memories over time? Viewing these processes through the lens of QIT could provide fresh perspectives and potential answers.

Technological Implications and Future Research

Beyond these theoretical considerations, QIT might also have practical implications. It could inspire new approaches to artificial intelligence and machine learning, leading to the creation of quantum neural networks that can outperform classical ones in certain tasks.

It might also pave the way for advanced neuroimaging techniques that can capture the brain's quantum dynamics in action, enhancing our ability to study brain function and disorders. Furthermore, understanding the quantum basis of neural processes could lead to novel therapies for neurological conditions.

Nonetheless, much work lies ahead. Establishing the role of quantum processes in the brain will require rigorous empirical testing, along with the development of viable theoretical models. Many researchers remain skeptical, given the brain's warm, wet, and noisy environment, which seems unfavorable for fragile quantum states. However, with ongoing advances in quantum biology, it's plausible that these hurdles could be overcome.

While the journey into the quantum realm of the brain is fraught with challenges and unknowns, the potential rewards are immense. As Quantum Information Theory continues to advance, we may find that it not only bridges the gap between neuroscience and holography but also provides a pathway to a deeper understanding of the mind and the nature of reality.

In the next part of this journey, we will delve into the intricacies of quantum cognition, a theory suggesting that quantum principles don't merely play a role at the neuronal level, but they also fundamentally shape our thought processes. It's a controversial idea, yet brimming with potential insights that could reshape our understanding of the mind.

As we delve deeper into the holographic mind, we find ourselves on the cusp of scientific frontiers, at the interface between the mind, the brain, and the universe beyond.

Quantum Cognition: A Quantum Leap in Understanding the Mind

As we continue our exploration of the holographic mind and the intersection of neuroscience and quantum physics, we arrive at a fascinating and provocative theory: quantum cognition. At its core, quantum cognition proposes that the mathematical principles of quantum mechanics are not just applicable to the world of tiny particles but can also provide a robust framework for understanding cognitive processes.

Quantum cognition does not suggest that the brain functions as a quantum computer, or that quantum physical phenomena occur in the brain, which is a separate field of research. Instead, it posits that the abstract mathematical machinery of quantum theory — developed to predict the behavior of light and matter at the minutest scales — can also be used to accurately model cognitive processes such as decision-making, perception, and memory.

Decision Making and Quantum Probability

One of the most compelling applications of quantum cognition is in the realm of decision-making. Classical theories of decision-making, rooted in classical probability theory, have long struggled with some peculiarities of human behavior.

Take, for instance, the violation of the 'sure-thing principle.' This principle, attributed to the 20th-century economist and Nobel laureate Paul Samuelson, holds that if you prefer option A to option B in one situation, and you also prefer option A to B in another situation, then you should prefer A to B even if you're uncertain about which situation applies.

However, this doesn't always hold in reality. In many instances, people's preferences change in response to the uncertainty, a phenomenon that conventional decision theories struggle to explain. But this behavior mirrors a fundamental aspect of quantum mechanics: the idea that a system can exist in multiple states simultaneously (superposition) and that the act of measuring the system can influence the state it adopts (collapse of the wave function).

Applying these principles, quantum cognition can elegantly account for the violation of the sure-thing principle. According to the quantum model, an individual's preferences can exist in a superposition of states, reflecting the inherent uncertainty in the decision-making process. When the person makes a decision, this superposition 'collapses' to a single state, just as a quantum system settles into a definite state when measured.

Perception, Memory, and Quantum Interference

Quantum cognition also offers fresh insights into other cognitive processes, such as perception and memory. For example, quantum models can explain the 'order effect,' where the sequence in which information is received affects an individual's perception or memory recall. This phenomenon resembles quantum interference, where the likelihood of a quantum particle following one path or another depends on the presence of alternative routes.

Moreover, quantum cognition can model the constructive nature of memory recall, where the act of remembering influences the memory itself. This mirrors the inherently interactive nature of quantum measurements, where observing a system can alter its state.

Challenges and Implications

Despite its promise, quantum cognition remains a fledgling field, and many questions are yet to be answered. Can quantum models accurately predict cognitive behavior in a wide range of scenarios, or are their successes limited to certain contexts? How can we test the predictions of quantum cognition against those of classical theories?

While we grapple with these questions, we must also consider the broader implications of quantum cognition. If our cognitive processes indeed mirror quantum phenomena, what does this say about the nature of the mind and reality? Can we leverage the principles of quantum cognition to develop more advanced artificial intelligence systems or to better understand the enigmatic phenomenon of consciousness?

In the chapters that follow, we'll delve into these questions, probing the frontiers of quantum cognition. Just as the hologram provides a richer, fuller representation of reality than a conventional photograph, so too might the quantum perspective offer a more complete understanding of the mind. As we journey deeper into the realm of quantum cognition, we're venturing into uncharted territory, exploring new dimensions of the mind that classical cognitive theories have yet to illuminate.

The interdisciplinary nature of quantum cognition also underscores the value of cross-pollination between fields. As physicists, neuroscientists, and cognitive scientists pool their insights, they're crafting a shared language to describe the mind — a language steeped in the fundamental principles of the universe.

Furthermore, the implications of quantum cognition extend beyond academia, touching on practical applications in various fields. For instance, in psychology, quantum models could provide a more nuanced understanding of human behavior, potentially informing interventions for mental health disorders. In computer science and artificial intelligence, quantum-inspired algorithms could lead to new machine learning techniques or problem-solving heuristics.

It's worth emphasizing that quantum cognition is not an end-point, but rather a stepping stone. As we press on in our exploration of the holographic mind, we will continually revisit and refine these models, integrating new discoveries and challenging our assumptions.

Quantum cognition, like any scientific theory, is a tool for thinking about the world. Its true power lies not in providing definitive answers, but in provoking new questions and offering fresh perspectives. It invites us to reconsider what we thought we knew about the mind and reality, to see familiar phenomena in a new light, and to wonder at the rich complexity of the human experience.

In the end, the greatest value of quantum cognition — and indeed, of the entire journey through the holographic mind — may be in the questions it inspires. How does the mind give rise to our subjective experience of reality? How does our perception of the world reflect the underlying nature of the universe? And how can we leverage these insights to enhance human well-being, to drive technological innovation, and to deepen our understanding of ourselves?

We stand at the threshold of an exciting frontier of knowledge, armed with a new set of tools to probe the enigma of the mind.

The holographic mind continues to yield fresh insights and raise fascinating questions, drawing us ever deeper into the mystery of consciousness and the universe. With each step, we're not only mapping uncharted territory but also charting a path for future explorations. As the story of the holographic mind unfolds, one thing is clear: the adventure is just beginning.

Interdisciplinary Approaches: The Roles of Computational Neuroscience and Artificial Intelligence

As we continue to chart the landscape of the holographic mind, it becomes increasingly apparent that a holistic understanding of such a complex phenomenon requires insights from multiple disciplines. Neuroscience provides the fundamental knowledge of the brain's structure and function, while quantum physics and holography offer innovative models for conceptualizing the mind. However, there are two other fields that are integral to our exploration: computational neuroscience and artificial intelligence (AI). These domains offer powerful tools for modeling the brain, elucidating cognitive processes, and potentially even simulating consciousness.

Computational Neuroscience: Building Bridges between Biology and Information

Computational neuroscience represents the convergence of biology, physics, mathematics, and computer science. It involves using computational models and simulations to understand the complex dynamics of the brain, from the interaction of individual neurons to the collective behavior of neural networks.

At its core, computational neuroscience seeks to unravel how the physical structure of the brain gives rise to its function—how billions of neurons interacting in a dense network can generate perceptions, emotions, and thoughts. By creating mathematical models of neurons and neural circuits, computational neuroscientists can simulate the brain's activity, make predictions, and generate hypotheses for further experimental testing.

One of the critical contributions of computational neuroscience to our understanding of the holographic mind is in the realm of neural networks. Traditional neuroscience provides detailed insights into the biology of neurons and synapses, but understanding how these components interact to create complex behaviors is a challenging task.

This is where the power of computational models comes in. They allow scientists to simulate large networks of neurons and observe their collective behavior. Some of these models incorporate the principles of holography, treating these neural networks as holographic systems. By adjusting the parameters of these models and comparing their output with empirical data, researchers can infer how real biological systems might operate.

In the context of our quantum holographic perspective, computational neuroscience can serve as a vital tool for testing hypotheses. For example, models can be designed to examine whether the dynamics of neural networks exhibit characteristics reminiscent of quantum systems, such as superposition or entanglement.

Artificial Intelligence: Simulating the Mind

Artificial Intelligence (AI) represents another powerful tool in our exploration of the holographic mind. At its heart, AI is about creating machines that can perform tasks requiring human-like intelligence, such as understanding natural language, recognizing patterns, solving problems, and learning from experience.

In essence, AI attempts to simulate aspects of human cognition. This process often involves creating algorithms inspired by our understanding of the brain. One notable example is artificial neural networks (ANNs), which are computational models designed to mimic the structure and function of biological neural networks.

ANNs have been instrumental in recent advances in AI, particularly in a subset called deep learning. These networks consist of multiple interconnected layers of artificial neurons, or nodes, which can process and transmit information in a manner analogous to biological neurons. Through a process of training and adjustment, these networks can learn to recognize patterns, make decisions, and even generate creative outputs.

What makes AI particularly relevant to our journey is its potential to shed light on the principles underlying cognition. By attempting to replicate aspects of human intelligence, AI researchers inadvertently reveal more about the nature of intelligence itself. How do we recognize patterns, understand language, or solve problems? By building machines that can perform these tasks, we learn more about these processes in humans.

In the context of the holographic mind, AI presents a tantalizing question: could we develop an AI that exhibits a form of holographic cognition? If so, it could serve as a powerful tool for understanding the mind and potentially even for exploring the nature of consciousness.

Intersecting Pathways: Computational Neuroscience and AI

There is a burgeoning intersection between computational neuroscience and AI, with each field informing the other, creating a symbiotic relationship that propels both forward. Computational neuroscience provides insights into how biological neural networks operate, offering inspiration for new AI algorithms and architectures. Conversely, AI provides tools for analyzing and interpreting the vast amounts of data generated by neuroscience research, and the successes (and failures) of AI can yield insights into human cognition.

Moreover, the convergence of these two fields offers a promising avenue for testing theories of the holographic mind. Could we develop computational models and AI systems that mimic proposed holographic neural processes? If such models were able to replicate human cognitive abilities more accurately or efficiently than traditional models, this could provide compelling evidence for the holographic mind.

Challenges and Future Directions

Despite the promise of computational neuroscience and AI, these fields are not without their challenges. One of the primary difficulties is the sheer complexity of the brain. Even the most powerful supercomputers are currently unable to simulate a human brain in its entirety, due to the vast number of neurons and synapses, and the complexity of their interactions.

In the realm of AI, one challenge lies in the so-called "black box" problem. While artificial neural networks can be trained to perform tasks with impressive accuracy, understanding how they reach their decisions can be challenging due to their complex and nonlinear nature. This lack of interpretability is a significant issue if we wish to use AI as a tool to understand human cognition.

Another challenge is the gap between AI and human cognitive abilities. Despite impressive advances in AI, even the most advanced systems are still far from matching the full range of human cognitive abilities. Moreover, while AI can mimic certain aspects of human intelligence, it does not inherently provide insight into the underlying processes — mimicry is not understanding.

However, these challenges should not dampen our enthusiasm but instead motivate further research. As we continue to refine our models and develop new methods, we move closer to the goal of understanding the brain and the mind.

As we journey through the vast expanse of the holographic mind, it becomes evident that computational neuroscience and AI are indispensable companions. They offer powerful tools for modeling the brain, elucidating cognitive processes, and potentially even simulating consciousness. In the world of computational neuroscience, we see the beauty of neural networks and their dynamic interactions, all elegantly captured in mathematical form. In the realm of AI, we see glimpses of human-like cognition in lines of code and computational structures, shedding light on the nature of intelligence.

Together, these fields invite us to view the brain and the mind from new perspectives, to see beyond the boundaries of traditional disciplines, and to imagine possibilities for understanding and even replicating cognition.

As we continue our exploration of the holographic mind, the tools and insights provided by computational neuroscience and AI will undoubtedly prove invaluable, helping us chart the contours of this uncharted terrain and guiding us towards new horizons in our understanding of the brain and the mind.

Future Visions: The Cutting Edge of Virtual Reality

The Emergence of Extended Reality (XR): Augmented, Mixed, and Virtual Realities

As we've journeyed through the realms of neuroscience, holography, and virtual reality, we've touched on revolutionary technologies and thought-provoking theories. Now, we will shift our gaze towards the horizon, exploring the exciting possibilities and nascent technologies that are shaping the future of our digital experiences. We're stepping into the era of Extended Reality (XR), a term that encapsulates Augmented Reality (AR), Mixed Reality (MR), and Virtual Reality (VR).

Augmented Reality: Merging the Digital and the Physical

Augmented reality overlays digital information onto the physical world. It allows users to interact with virtual content in their real surroundings, seamlessly integrating digital information with the user's environment in real-time. AR is like a bridge connecting our physical reality and the digital realm, enhancing our perception and interaction with the world around us.

AR technology has been making its mark in numerous fields. In education, it's being used to make learning more interactive and engaging, bringing subjects to life in ways that textbooks can't. In healthcare, AR applications can help surgeons visualize complex procedures or assist patients in physical therapy. In retail, AR apps can let consumers virtually try on clothes, makeup, or see how furniture might look in their home.

Emerging trends in AR are pointing towards increasingly immersive experiences. Technologies like Light Field Displays can project 3D holograms into the real world, providing a more immersive form of AR that can be viewed from different angles. Another exciting development is the advent of AR wearables, such as smart glasses, which could potentially revolutionize how we consume digital information in our everyday lives.

Mixed Reality: When Real and Virtual Worlds Collide

While AR overlays digital information onto the real world, Mixed Reality takes it a step further by allowing real and virtual objects to coexist and interact in real-time. MR blends the physical and digital worlds into new hybrid environments where physical and digital objects coexist and interact in real time.

MR technologies like Microsoft's HoloLens provide a tantalizing glimpse into the potential of this technology. These devices allow users to place and interact with holographic items in their physical surroundings. Imagine designing a room by placing virtual furniture, or collaborating with colleagues on a 3D project, manipulating the model in real-time.

However, the promise of MR extends beyond holograms. One exciting frontier is the idea of spatial computing, where our interactions with computers break free from the constraints of screens and become integrated with our physical environment. In this vision of the future, the whole world becomes a canvas for digital information.

Virtual Reality: Immersive Alternate Realities

Virtual reality, on the other hand, offers a completely immersive experience that shuts out the physical world. Using VR devices such as headsets, users can be transported into a number of real-world and imagined environments. It's a technology that, at its ultimate, promises to transcend physical boundaries and transform how we experience digital content.

Over the years, VR technology has seen significant advancements. From the development of room-scale VR to the introduction of haptic feedback technology, VR has become more immersive and interactive. The next frontier for VR could be incorporating more of our senses into the VR experience. Imagine a VR system that not only lets you see and hear a digital environment but also smell, taste, and touch it.

The Convergence of Realities

At the heart of all these technologies lies the idea of creating more natural, intuitive ways of interacting with digital information. By blending the physical and digital worlds, XR technologies can provide more immersive, engaging experiences that push the boundaries of storytelling, communication, work, and play.

However, XR also presents new challenges and opportunities for our understanding of the brain and cognition. As we create technologies that provide more immersive and holistic experiences, we're also creating new ways to engage and stimulate the brain. XR technologies have the potential to enhance cognitive abilities, foster new forms of communication, and even create new types of sensory experiences. In a way, XR technologies can be seen as a new frontier in our ongoing exploration of the holographic mind.

XR could also have profound implications for fields such as neuroscience and psychology. As these technologies become more prevalent, we will inevitably learn more about how our brains respond to these blended realities. We will learn how our perception is affected when physical and digital elements coexist and interact in the same space, how our cognitive processes are influenced when we can manipulate digital objects just like physical ones, and how our brains adapt when faced with entirely new sensory experiences.

One emerging area of research is studying the therapeutic potential of XR. For instance, VR has been used to treat conditions such as PTSD and phobias through exposure therapy. By creating a safe, controlled environment, therapists can gradually expose patients to their fears, helping them to overcome them. XR can also be used for physical rehabilitation. For example, AR and VR can transform mundane physical therapy exercises into engaging games, encouraging patients to stick with their treatment.

The Future of Extended Reality

Looking forward, the boundaries between AR, MR, and VR will continue to blur as these technologies advance and converge. We're heading towards a future where we seamlessly transition between interacting with digital information on physical surfaces, blending physical and digital elements in our environment, and immersing ourselves in completely digital worlds. The idea of separate "realities" might become obsolete, replaced by a fluid, continuous spectrum of experiences.

One key factor in this future will be the development of smart glasses or even contact lenses capable of AR, MR, and VR. These devices will need to be comfortable to wear, offer high-quality visuals, and be equipped with advanced features like eye tracking, spatial audio, and hand tracking. They will need to be powerful enough to render complex 3D scenes, yet efficient enough to have a reasonable battery life

Moreover, we'll need new types of interfaces for interacting with XR environments. These might include gestural interfaces, voice commands, haptic feedback devices, and even brain-computer interfaces.

Lastly, in the future, XR experiences will likely be powered by technologies like 5G and edge computing, which can provide the high bandwidth and low latency needed for seamless, real-time experiences. Artificial intelligence will also play a significant role, powering everything from voice recognition to real-time object detection and tracking.

As we stand on the brink of the XR era, we are also on the verge of a new chapter in our understanding of the mind. The technologies we create reflect our understanding of how we perceive and interact with the world, but they also shape our understanding. As we develop and interact with XR technologies, we will not only be pushing the boundaries of what's possible in digital experiences, but we'll also be exploring the frontiers of the holographic mind, learning more about how our brains create and interact with reality, whether physical or digital, real or imagined.

Empathetic AI and Immersive Storytelling: Building Emotional Connections in VR

In the realm of virtual reality (VR), we've explored vast, intricate landscapes and embarked on countless journeys. Yet, as we delve deeper into this technological marvel, we find that the future of VR isn't just about sight and sound, touch and motion—it's about emotion.

The most profound, moving experiences are those that make us feel. They engage our hearts, stir our emotions, and leave us transformed. The frontier of VR development is no different. By harnessing the power of empathetic Artificial Intelligence (AI) and leveraging immersive storytelling, we're venturing into an era where digital experiences are not only realistic but resonate on an emotional level. Welcome to the brave new world of emotional connections in VR.

Empathetic AI: Giving a Heart to the Machine

In its essence, empathetic AI is about creating machines that understand and respond to human emotions. By incorporating principles of psychology, cognitive science, and machine learning, empathetic AI aims to imbue our digital companions with a level of emotional intelligence that enhances our interactions and engenders a sense of connection and understanding.

Imagine a virtual companion that can gauge your mood by analyzing your voice tone, facial expressions, or even physiological signals like heart rate or skin conductance. It could then respond in a way that reflects an understanding of your emotional state, providing comfort when you're sad, sharing your excitement when you're happy, or offering encouragement when you're frustrated.

Yet, empathetic AI goes beyond mere detection and reaction—it's about engagement and interaction. It's about building an AI system that can participate in the ebb and flow of human emotions, fostering a bond between human and machine that is dynamic, responsive, and deeply personal.

Immersive Storytelling: A New Narrative Paradigm

Traditionally, storytelling has been a linear experience, with the audience passively receiving a narrative crafted by the author. In contrast, immersive storytelling empowers the audience to actively participate in the narrative, exploring the story world, interacting with characters, and influencing the course of events.

In VR, immersive storytelling takes on a whole new dimension. You're not just observing the story—you're living it. You can step into the shoes of the protagonist, make decisions that shape the narrative, and engage with the story world in a visceral, tactile way. It's a new narrative paradigm that blurs the line between story and reality, creating an emotional and experiential depth that traditional media can't match.

Building Emotional Connections in VR: The Intersection of Empathetic AI and Immersive Storytelling

Empathetic AI and immersive storytelling, when integrated into VR, open the door to deeply engaging experiences that evoke genuine emotion and foster meaningful connections. The immersive nature of VR allows users to step into a narrative, while empathetic AI brings the story world to life, creating emotionally responsive characters and environments.

Consider a VR narrative that incorporates an empathetic AI system. As you explore the story world, the characters you encounter aren't just scripted NPCs (Non-Player Characters)—they're emotionally intelligent beings capable of understanding and responding to your feelings. They notice if you're hesitant or excited, offer comfort if you're distressed, and react appropriately to your choices and actions.

Moreover, the story world itself can be emotionally responsive. The environment could reflect the narrative's emotional tone, shifting its visual style, music, and ambient sounds based on the story's progression and your emotional state. Imagine a scene that brightens and fills with soft, uplifting music when you experience joy, or darkens and grows silent during moments of tension or fear.

This integration of empathetic AI and immersive storytelling in VR can lead to transformative experiences. These narratives could elicit a wide spectrum of emotions and provide a sense of agency that traditional media can't match. With empathetic AI, the narrative is no longer a fixed sequence of events but a living, breathing entity that understands and resonates with your emotional state. It adapts and evolves based on your actions, creating a deeply personal journey that is unique to you.

Furthermore, this technology could usher in a new era of empathetic digital companions. Picture a VR experience where your AI companion shares in your adventures, reacts to your emotions, and evolves over time. This companion could be a friend, mentor, or even a digital pet, offering emotional support and companionship in a way that is both engaging and emotionally fulfilling.

Empathetic AI, Immersive Storytelling, and the Holographic Mind

But what does this all mean for our understanding of the holographic mind? As we interact with empathetic AI and immersive narratives in VR, we are effectively engaging with complex, dynamic systems that reflect and respond to our emotions and actions. This interaction creates a feedback loop that mirrors the holographic nature of our brain, where each part is interconnected and influences the whole.

The emotional bonds we form with AI companions and the emotional journeys we undertake in immersive narratives stimulate our brains in a holistic, interconnected manner. We are not just processing visual or auditory information—we are engaging our emotions, our memories, and our sense of self. This comprehensive, all-encompassing engagement could potentially activate our brains in a way that closely mirrors the holographic principle, providing a new, immersive avenue for exploring and understanding the nature of our minds.

Looking Ahead: The Future of Empathetic AI and Immersive Storytelling in VR

As we move forward, the role of empathetic AI and immersive storytelling in VR will continue to grow. We'll see more sophisticated AI that can better understand and respond to a broader range of human emotions. We'll encounter more immersive narratives that offer richer, more diverse experiences. And as these technologies evolve, we'll have the opportunity to explore new aspects of the holographic mind, deepening our understanding of this fascinating principle.

Moreover, we'll see these technologies expand beyond entertainment and into areas like education, healthcare, and social connectivity. Imagine VR learning experiences where empathetic AI tutors adapt their teaching style based on your emotional state or VR therapy sessions where empathetic AI therapists provide comfort and support. Imagine VR social platforms where you can share immersive stories with friends and family, fostering a sense of connection and empathy even when you're miles apart.

In the end, the marriage of empathetic AI and immersive storytelling in VR promises to not only revolutionize our digital experiences but also bring us closer to understanding the complex, beautiful mystery of our minds. And as we step into this brave new world of emotional connections in VR, we embark on a journey that will forever change our perception of reality and our relationship with technology.

And this is not just the realm of pure speculation. With every passing day, we're making strides towards turning these visions into reality. The cutting-edge research in neuroscience, AI, and VR are converging to give us a glimpse of this exciting future, bringing us closer to the day when we can fully explore and understand the wonders of the holographic mind.

Neurofeedback in VR: Personalizing Experiences through Brainwave Data

We stand at a crossroads in technological history where the possibilities of merging neuroscience and virtual reality (VR) are beginning to manifest as tangible, practical applications. One such intersection is the burgeoning field of neurofeedback in VR. By harnessing brainwave data, we can further personalize VR experiences, paving the way for therapeutic interventions, optimized learning environments, and emotionally resonant narratives.

What is Neurofeedback?

Before diving into the applications in VR, it's helpful to understand the basics of neurofeedback. In essence, neurofeedback is a type of biofeedback that uses real-time displays of brain activity to self-regulate brain functions. Electroencephalography (EEG) is often used to monitor brainwave patterns, providing immediate feedback to the user. This feedback can guide the individual to make conscious changes to their brainwave patterns, thereby influencing mood, focus, stress levels, and more.

Neurofeedback has been used in various settings, from treating conditions such as ADHD and PTSD, to improving the performance of athletes and musicians. The real-time aspect of neurofeedback allows individuals to understand their current brain state, helping them learn how to modulate their brainwaves to achieve desired outcomes.

The Convergence of Neurofeedback and VR

The real-time, immersive nature of VR makes it a perfect platform for neurofeedback. In a VR setting, neurofeedback can be integrated seamlessly into the user's experience, providing an immediate and visceral representation of one's brain state.

For example, consider a calming VR environment, such as a serene forest or a tranquil beach. The ambiance—visuals, sounds, even smells if olfactory technology is incorporated—changes based on your brainwave data. If you're stressed, the weather in your VR world might turn cloudy. As you relax, the sun emerges. This feedback loop, presented in an engaging, immersive manner, allows you to visualize your internal state and, over time, learn to control it.

Therapeutic Applications

Neurofeedback in VR holds significant promise in therapeutic contexts. For people dealing with stress, anxiety, or post-traumatic stress disorder (PTSD), a personalized VR environment can serve as a safe space for relaxation and recovery.

Picture a VR therapeutic program designed for stress relief. The program uses real-time EEG data to assess your stress levels and adjusts the VR environment accordingly. If your brainwave patterns indicate high stress, the VR landscape might display a turbulent ocean. As you employ relaxation techniques, the seas become calm. Over time, you learn to control your stress response, with the VR environment acting as a mirror of your internal state.

Optimized Learning Environments

On the education front, neurofeedback in VR can create optimized learning environments that adapt to a student's mental state. If the student is distracted or overwhelmed, the VR learning program can respond in real-time, adjusting the pace of instruction, modifying the complexity of the material, or suggesting a break.

Imagine a VR classroom that can interpret a student's focus level based on EEG data. If the student's attention starts to wane, the classroom environment could change—perhaps the lights dim, or the virtual instructor switches to a more engaging teaching method. This personalization can optimize the learning process, ensuring that each student receives instruction that aligns with their current cognitive state.

Immersive and Adaptive Storytelling

For the entertainment industry, neurofeedback can create emotionally resonant and highly personalized narratives. Interactive VR experiences can be made even more immersive by adjusting the narrative flow, character interactions, and environmental settings based on the user's emotional state.

Envision an interactive VR story that uses neurofeedback to personalize the narrative. If you're engaged and excited, the story might ramp up the action. If you're overwhelmed, the narrative might slow down, providing space for reflection or lower-intensity interaction. Such a system could truly deliver a unique story for each user, tailored to their emotional responses.

Brain-Computer Interfaces and Neurofeedback

The emerging field of brain-computer interfaces (BCIs) also plays a crucial role in the evolution of neurofeedback in VR. BCIs provide a direct communication pathway between the brain and an external device, typically through EEG. High-profile ventures, such as Neuralink by Elon Musk, have brought BCIs into public awareness, though most current applications are medical. However, as BCIs become more sophisticated and accessible, they could become integral to VR, enabling more precise neurofeedback.

With a BCI, the potential for personalization in VR expands exponentially. It could be possible to control VR environments or avatars simply by thinking about it, with the BCI translating brainwave patterns into commands. This development could enhance the VR experience in gaming, social interactions, professional collaborations, and more.

The Potential and Challenges Ahead

While the convergence of neurofeedback and VR presents exciting possibilities, it's important to remember that we're still in the early stages of this journey. Challenges related to data privacy, ethical considerations around brain data, and technical hurdles, such as improving the precision of non-invasive BCIs, are all areas that require careful consideration and research.

Furthermore, while personalization is a significant benefit of integrating neurofeedback and VR, it also introduces the question of how to ensure a balanced, beneficial experience for the user. If a VR environment constantly adapts to a user's current brain state, could there be instances where it inadvertently reinforces negative states? Developers will need to approach these issues with care and insight, perhaps integrating safeguards to ensure the technology promotes overall wellbeing.

On a broader scale, integrating neurofeedback in VR aligns with our ongoing exploration of the holographic mind. The real-time, interactive feedback provided by neurofeedback mirrors the dynamic, interconnected nature of our brains. As we learn to modulate our brainwave patterns within VR environments, we engage with our brains in a way that reflects the holographic principle—where the part influences the whole and the whole influences the part.

Ultimately, the marriage of neurofeedback and VR opens up exciting new frontiers in our understanding of the mind, our approach to mental health, education, and entertainment.

As we continue to navigate this uncharted territory, we move closer to realizing the full potential of this transformative intersection of neuroscience and technology. The exploration of these realms not only enriches our present but also provides a tantalizing glimpse into the future of human potential.

This is the vision that guides the next steps on our path: a future where VR experiences are intimately tied to our cognition, where we can visualize and guide our internal states, and where our understanding of the brain and mind expands through these unique, immersive journeys.

It's a testament to our enduring quest for self-understanding and an affirmation of our potential to reshape our realities—virtual and otherwise—through the power of the mind.

Part III: Intersections and Implications

When Mind Meets Matrix: The Intersection of Holographic Mind Theory and Virtual Reality

When we set out to explore the concept of the holographic mind, we embarked on a journey across the uncharted terrains of quantum physics, neuroscience, and virtual reality. Now, we find ourselves at a fascinating crossroads where these distinct fields converge. This intersection, where the theory of the holographic mind meets the immersive realms of virtual reality, opens up vast vistas of untapped potential and unexplored possibilities.

Understanding the holographic mind theory, as we have discussed, involves embracing the idea that each part of the brain contains the whole of its information—a departure from the conventional viewpoint that different mental processes are localized in specific regions. This theory underpins our exploration of brain functioning and cognition in a more holistic, integrative manner.

Virtual reality, on the other hand, transports us into immersive digital realms, where the only limit to what we can experience is our imagination. Through the veil of VR, we can interact with digital environments as though they were tangible, creating a suspension of disbelief that blurs the boundary between the real and the virtual.

So, what happens when we apply the holographic principle to VR? Can we create a virtual representation of our mental processes that goes beyond simple avatars and into the complex webs of thoughts, memories, and emotions? Let's venture into these unexplored intersections.

Simulating the Holographic Mind: Can VR Model our Mental Processes?

Translating the holographic mind theory into a tangible VR model presents an intriguing challenge. It's akin to mapping an uncharted territory—a territory that is not geographical but cognitive and experiential. Our mental processes aren't linear sequences that can be easily rendered into a digital format. They are fluid, dynamic, and deeply interconnected, much like the shifting, ripple-like patterns of a hologram.

To model our mental processes, we'd need a VR environment that mirrors the brain's holographic nature— one that's dynamic, adaptable, and capable of representing the intricate links between different cognitive functions. This would be a significant leap beyond our current VR capabilities, which typically focus on creating visually immersive environments.

Yet, the concept isn't entirely out of reach. Imagine a VR simulation that represents your thought processes as a sprawling, three-dimensional web. Each strand of the web represents a different cognitive function—memory, emotion, perception, etc. When you engage in a specific cognitive task, the relevant strands light up, creating a luminous pathway that reflects your thought process. As different cognitive functions interact and influence each other, the web shifts and adapts, mirroring the dynamic, interconnected nature of your cognition.

Beyond visual representation, this VR model could potentially provide a form of neurofeedback, helping you understand and regulate your cognitive processes. Seeing your thought processes played out in an immersive VR environment could promote greater self-awareness and facilitate cognitive control.

Furthermore, this technology could serve as a powerful tool for psychological therapy, education, and cognitive research. Therapists could gain insights into their clients' cognitive patterns, students could better understand complex concepts, and researchers could observe mental processes in real time.

However, we must tread with caution. The simulation of our mental processes in VR raises a myriad of ethical and philosophical questions. What are the implications of having a digital representation of our innermost thoughts and feelings? Who would have access to these VR models? How would we ensure the responsible use of such intimate data? These are questions that we must address as we venture further into the intersection of holographic mind theory and virtual reality.

The journey into this crossroads of neuroscience and technology is undoubtedly challenging, filled with intricate puzzles and deep-rooted questions. However, it's a path we must traverse for it holds the potential to revolutionize our understanding of the human mind and transform our interaction with digital environments. As we delve deeper into this intersection, we may unlock new dimensions of cognition, forge a more intimate connection with our mental processes, and glean a greater understanding of our holographic mind.

In this respect, brain-computer interfaces and AI could play significant roles, not only in creating these VR simulations but also in decoding and translating the complex language of our brainwaves into an understandable format. The incorporation of AI could facilitate the adaptive, responsive nature of the VR model, allowing it to change and grow in sync with our evolving cognitive patterns.

Equally important is the role of computational neuroscience, which could provide the foundational knowledge required to create an accurate and comprehensive VR model of the mind. By drawing on computational models of how neurons and neural networks function, we could start to build a VR model that mirrors these processes in a tangible, visual format.

Yet, we also need to consider the potential effects of prolonged VR use on our mental health and cognition. Immersing ourselves in VR environments can influence our perception, cognition, and neural functioning. As we spend more time in these digital realms, we may need to consider how this can affect our brains. Do our minds start to adapt to the VR environment? Does our cognition start to mirror the virtual rather than the real?

Understanding these potential effects could help us strike a balance between the virtual and the real, ensuring that VR remains a tool for enhancing our understanding of the mind, rather than a substitute for our tangible reality.

Moreover, as we continue to explore the intersection of the holographic mind and VR, we must remember to keep our ethical compass in sight. As mentioned earlier, the simulation of mental processes in VR can yield deeply personal, sensitive data. Ensuring the responsible use and secure storage of this data should be of utmost priority.

As we stand at this intersection, we're not just looking at the convergence of theories and technologies; we're looking at a convergence of opportunities and challenges, of tangible benefits and ethical considerations. We're at a crossroads where our thirst for knowledge meets our responsibility as scientists, researchers, and ethical beings. It's an exhilarating, thought-provoking journey—one that promises to shed new light on the labyrinthine mystery of the human mind and the myriad ways in which we perceive and interact with our realities, both real and virtual.

We have now woven together the threads of holography, quantum mechanics, neuroscience, and virtual reality into a compelling tapestry that explores the multifaceted nature of the mind. Our journey into the holographic mind is far from over. The horizon is still teeming with questions, each one a stepping stone towards deeper understanding and novel discoveries. As we stride forth into this untamed landscape, let us continue to explore, question, and marvel at the complexity and elegance of the human mind—the most intricate and fascinating hologram of all.

Experiencing Consciousness: A New Approach to Understanding the Mind

Stepping into the realm of consciousness, we embark on an exploration that, in many ways, is as profound and complex as any journey through the furthest reaches of the cosmos. But here, we're not dealing with stars and galaxies, but rather with the very essence of what it means to be a sentient being. Consciousness – the sense of self-awareness, the experience of one's existence – is, without a doubt, one of the most intriguing and elusive phenomena we encounter.

To understand consciousness, we need to take a multi-disciplinary approach. We need to traverse the pathways of neuroscience, psychology, philosophy, quantum physics, and yes, holography and virtual reality. It's at this nexus that we can perhaps gain a fresh perspective, a novel way of understanding consciousness.

The Holographic Consciousness

The holographic mind theory, as we've discussed, suggests that our brains function much like a hologram, encoding and processing information in a distributed, non-localized manner. Could this holographic principle also extend to our consciousness?

Consider the nature of a hologram. Every part contains the whole. Shift your perspective, and the image changes, revealing new aspects of the entire object. In a similar vein, our consciousness may be akin to this dynamic, interconnected web, where every thought, sensation, and perception contains a piece of our overall conscious experience. As we navigate through this web, we continuously reshape and redefine our experience of consciousness.

The Consciousness Matrix

If we extend this idea further and merge it with the realms of virtual reality, we might conceive of a consciousness matrix – a VR model that represents our conscious experiences. In this matrix, each data point, each node represents a facet of our consciousness – a memory, a thought, an emotion, a sensory experience. Together, they create a dynamic, multi-dimensional matrix that represents the complexity and interconnectedness of our consciousness.

Creating such a matrix would be a monumental task. It would necessitate not just advanced VR technology, but also profound insights into the nature of consciousness itself – insights that we are only just beginning to uncover. Furthermore, it would require a mechanism to accurately and reliably translate our conscious experiences into a digital format – a task that seems almost insurmountable given the deeply subjective and elusive nature of consciousness.

A New Approach to Understanding the Mind

Nonetheless, this concept of a consciousness matrix offers a fresh perspective on how we might approach understanding the mind. Rather than treating the mind as a static entity, we begin to see it as a dynamic, ever-evolving landscape. Our conscious experiences are not isolated events, but rather intricately connected facets of a larger whole.

Moreover, by viewing consciousness through the lens of holography and virtual reality, we can begin to appreciate its complexity and nuance. We see that it's not merely a byproduct of brain activity, but a rich tapestry of experiences that reflects our interactions with the world around us.

The immersive nature of virtual reality could provide a platform for exploring and experiencing this dynamic landscape in a tangible, experiential way. In a sense, VR could serve as a kind of consciousness microscope, allowing us to delve into the intricate details of our conscious experiences and explore them from a first-person perspective.

Just as a microscope allows us to see the minute details of a cell, so too could a VR-based consciousness matrix help us understand the nuances of our conscious experiences. Imagine being able to navigate through your memories, emotions, and thoughts, observing them from different angles, understanding their interconnectedness, and gaining insight into how they shape your overall conscious experience.

Implications and Considerations

However, as we explore this new approach to understanding the mind, we must also be mindful of its implications. Simulating consciousness within a virtual environment raises profound ethical and philosophical questions. If we can replicate the mind's inner workings accurately, do these digital recreations possess consciousness themselves? Are we simply observers in this digital consciousness landscape, or do we become active participants in the shaping and molding of our conscious experiences?

We must also address the issue of privacy and personal boundaries. Our consciousness is our most intimate space. If we are to digitize our conscious experiences, we need robust measures to ensure the security and integrity of this deeply personal data. This concern is not just about the potential misuse of the information. It also pertains to how our experiences, once digitized, might change our perception of our own consciousness. Does a virtual representation of our consciousness alter our understanding and relationship with our own mind?

Moreover, we need to consider the potential psychological impacts. How would the ability to view our conscious experiences from a third-person perspective affect us? While it might offer valuable insights, it could also lead to an unsettling sense of detachment or dissociation.

A Gateway to Discovery

Despite these challenges, the prospect of a VR-based consciousness matrix is undeniably exciting. It presents a new gateway to understanding one of the most profound and complex aspects of human existence. It proposes a framework that combines quantum physics, neuroscience, psychology, holography, and cutting-edge technology to explore the labyrinth of the mind.

Ultimately, the exploration of consciousness through the holographic mind theory and VR is about pushing the boundaries of our understanding. It's about seeking a new language – a language of interconnectivity, immersion, and dynamism – to describe and comprehend the experience of being aware.

The journey toward understanding consciousness is a delicate balance between science and philosophy, between data and introspection, between objectivity and subjectivity. It is, at its core, a deeply human endeavor—one that calls upon us to explore not just the outer world, but also our inner universes.

As we venture forth in this bold exploration, we need to retain a sense of humility and wonder. For even as we strive to map out the terrain of consciousness, we must never lose sight of its mystery, its depth, its sheer inexplicability. It is this sense of awe that drives us forward, igniting our curiosity and fueling our quest for knowledge.

In our quest to understand consciousness, we are not merely dissecting a scientific phenomenon. We are unraveling the very essence of what it means to be human. And in this endeavor, we find not just answers, but also questions – questions that challenge us, that provoke us, and that inspire us to continue our exploration.

Cognitive Empathy in VR: Understanding Others' Minds through Immersive Experiences

The great philosopher Plato once said, "Be kind, for everyone you meet is fighting a hard battle." This call for empathy, for the capacity to understand and share the feelings of another, is as critical today as it was over two millennia ago. In an increasingly interconnected world, empathy forms the bedrock of our social interactions and communal bonds. It is a cornerstone of our humanity.

As we delve into the digital age, virtual reality (VR) presents a novel approach to cultivating empathy. Can VR, a technology that immerses us in alternate realities, help us better understand the realities of others? Let's delve into this fascinating intersection of empathy, VR, and cognition.

Empathy and its Cognitive Dimension

Empathy, in its broadest sense, involves two main components: emotional empathy, where we share and respond to others' feelings, and cognitive empathy, where we understand and appreciate others' perspectives. Our focus here is cognitive empathy, the mental process of stepping into someone else's shoes and viewing the world from their standpoint.

Cognitive empathy doesn't necessarily involve sharing the emotions of the other person, but rather comprehending their emotional state and their thought processes. It's the understanding that if we were in their place, with their experiences and worldview, we might feel and think the same way.

Virtual Reality: A Platform for Empathy

Now, where does VR fit into this? Virtual reality's unique selling point is its immersive nature – it has the power to transport users into different environments, circumstances, even bodies, all while delivering a convincing sense of 'presence'. VR can simulate not just what it looks like to be in someone else's shoes, but what it feels like, sounds like, and perhaps even smells like.

By leveraging this immersive capacity, VR can serve as an 'empathy machine', allowing users to experience alternate realities that mirror the experiences of others. This could range from experiencing the daily challenges faced by an individual with a disability, to understanding the hardships endured by refugees fleeing conflict, to appreciating the struggles of individuals battling mental health issues.

Cognitive Empathy in Action: VR Scenarios

Imagine, for instance, a VR simulation that lets you experience life with a visual impairment. As you navigate this virtual world, you encounter the obstacles, inconveniences, and challenges faced by visually impaired individuals daily. You experience the frustration, the struggle, and the adaptations required. This immersive experience could foster a deeper understanding, a cognitive empathy, for the challenges such individuals face.

Similarly, a VR scenario could immerse you in the life of a refugee. You'd endure the fear, the uncertainty, the hardship. You'd face the tough choices, experience the loss, feel the desperation. By placing you in these circumstances, VR could cultivate cognitive empathy, fostering an understanding of the refugee experience that goes beyond what's possible through traditional media.

Empathetic AI: Adding Depth to VR Experiences

Advancements in AI, particularly in empathetic AI, can further enhance these VR experiences. Empathetic AI, designed to understand and respond to human emotions, could adapt the VR scenario based on your reactions, creating a more personalized, dynamic experience.
For instance, if the AI detects signs of stress or confusion during a VR experience, it could provide additional information or guidance. Conversely, if the AI observes signs of complacency or indifference, it could intensify the scenario to elicit a stronger empathetic response.

This combination of VR and empathetic AI could create powerful, immersive experiences that drive cognitive empathy, fostering a deeper understanding of the diverse range of human experiences.

The Ethical Considerations of Empathy in VR

While VR's potential to foster cognitive empathy is exciting, it also raises critical ethical considerations. The ability to simulate others' experiences is a powerful tool, but it's also a significant responsibility. VR developers must ensure these experiences are authentic, respectful, and sensitive to the realities they're depicting. They must avoid oversimplification or sensationalization, which could lead to misconceptions or reinforce stereotypes.

Moreover, VR experiences intended to foster empathy must be designed with care to avoid causing distress or harm. It's crucial to strike a balance between creating an impactful experience and ensuring the mental and emotional safety of users. The integration of empathetic AI can be pivotal here, allowing for personalized experiences that adapt to users' responses.

Furthermore, users need to understand the limitations of these VR experiences. While VR can simulate aspects of others' experiences, it can't fully replicate them. Users must be mindful that these experiences are just a glimpse into others' realities, not a comprehensive understanding.

Shaping a More Empathetic Future with VR

Cognitive empathy plays a crucial role in fostering understanding, compassion, and social cohesion. As our world becomes more interconnected and diverse, the importance of empathy is only going to grow. In this context, VR's potential to enhance cognitive empathy is not just a technological novelty. It's a tool for social progress.

By offering immersive experiences that simulate others' realities, VR can help us comprehend the breadth and depth of human experiences. It can remind us of our shared humanity, of our capacity for understanding and compassion. In doing so, it can help us bridge divides, challenge biases, and foster a more empathetic, inclusive society.

In the realms of education, healthcare, social work, and beyond, VR's potential to foster cognitive empathy is immense. As we continue to explore and refine this potential, we must do so with care, respect, and a commitment to authenticity.

Looking ahead, the future of VR as an empathy machine seems both promising and challenging. With continued technological advancements, the ethical guidance of experts, and thoughtful design, VR could become a potent tool in our quest for a more understanding, empathetic world.

As we harness the power of VR for cognitive empathy, we're not just adopting a new technology. We're embarking on a journey of understanding, of seeing the world through others' eyes, and perhaps, in the process, learning a bit more about ourselves. It's a journey that holds the promise of a more empathetic, more compassionate, and more understanding society.

With VR, we are creating more than just simulations. We're creating opportunities for insight, empathy, and transformation. Let's strive to do so with mindfulness, with respect for the realities we're depicting, and with a deep-seated commitment to fostering understanding and empathy. After all, as we step into others' virtual shoes, we're not just exploring their realities—we're also shaping our own.

The Ethical Frontier: Navigating the Implications of a Holographic Mind and VR

Ethical Challenges of Understanding the Holographic Mind

Our exploration into the holographic mind and the advent of virtual reality (VR) technologies raises profound ethical questions. As we stand at the precipice of a new era, where the intersection of neuroscience and VR could redefine our understanding of consciousness and personal identity, it is important that we anticipate and navigate these ethical challenges with care, diligence, and foresight.

Privacy and Consent in a Brain-Interfaced World

The holographic mind theory suggests a model of human cognition where information is distributed across the brain, much like a hologram, rather than localized to specific regions. This theory, if verified, could revolutionize our approach to understanding and interacting with the human mind. However, the potential to access and manipulate this distributed cognition network introduces significant privacy concerns.

In a world where technology can decode our thought patterns and potentially interact with them, the question of consent becomes paramount. If we can access a person's thoughts or emotions through brain-computer interfaces, what safeguards must be in place to ensure their privacy? Will there be a need for "cognitive consent," and how will it be obtained and maintained?

Responsible Use of Cognitive Data

Additionally, the acquisition and use of cognitive data must be performed responsibly. Just as personal data is protected by laws and regulations, cognitive data, too, should be subject to strict guidelines. The misuse or unauthorized access to cognitive data could lead to substantial harm, such as cognitive hacking, manipulation, or unauthorized profiling.

This raises questions about the ownership and control of cognitive data. Should individuals retain exclusive rights to their cognitive data, much like they do with their personal and medical information? Furthermore, should they be given the right to opt-out of cognitive data collection altogether?

Impact on Human Identity and Perception

On a deeper level, the convergence of the holographic mind theory and VR challenges our very conception of personal identity and reality. If our minds can be modelled like a hologram, and if VR can create experiences virtually indistinguishable from reality, where do we draw the line between the virtual and the real, the self and the other?

Such blurring of boundaries could have profound implications for our sense of self and our understanding of reality. As we navigate this ethical frontier, we must carefully consider the psychological and societal implications of these technologies and their potential impact on human identity and perception.

Shaping an Ethical Framework

Confronting these ethical challenges requires a multidisciplinary approach, combining insights from neuroscience, philosophy, computer science, law, and ethics. A robust ethical framework must be established, ensuring the responsible development and use of technologies related to the holographic mind and VR.

The framework should incorporate principles of transparency, accountability, privacy, and respect for autonomy. It should also address issues of equity and accessibility, ensuring that the benefits of these technologies are available to all, without exacerbating social inequalities.

Moreover, it is essential to foster an ongoing dialogue between scientists, technologists, ethicists, policymakers, and the public. This collective conversation can help us navigate the ethical frontier, ensuring we harness the potential of these technologies while safeguarding our fundamental values and rights.

While the intersection of the holographic mind theory and VR promises exciting possibilities, it also raises profound ethical challenges. As we venture into this new frontier, it is our responsibility to ensure that we navigate it ethically, with respect for individual rights and the collective good. Only then can we fully harness the potential of these technologies, transforming our understanding of the mind and reality, without compromising our fundamental human values.

Digital Wellbeing in Virtual Environments: Ethical Concerns and Best Practices

As we traverse the frontier of integrating the holographic mind theory with virtual reality (VR), it becomes paramount to focus on maintaining digital wellbeing in virtual environments. This novel concept expands on the existing paradigm of digital wellbeing – traditionally concerned with healthy practices around digital media use, screen time, and online etiquette – to incorporate the unique challenges posed by immersive virtual experiences. Here, we delve into the ethical concerns associated with digital wellbeing in VR, while also proposing best practices to safeguard users' mental and emotional health.

Ethical Concerns

1. Virtual Derealization and Depersonalization

Derealization and depersonalization refer to the sensations of feeling detached from one's self and surroundings, feeling as though you or the world around you is not real.

These phenomena, commonly associated with certain mental health disorders, could become more prevalent as VR experiences become more immersive. The lines between virtual and actual reality could blur, causing distress, confusion, and other psychological issues.

2. Privacy and Identity

As discussed in the previous section, the intersection of holographic mind theory and VR raises privacy concerns that go beyond traditional digital spaces. In a virtual environment, a person's behavior, interactions, even their gaze can be tracked and analyzed, potentially leading to a level of surveillance and intrusion of privacy never before experienced. The manipulation of these data points could lead to identity theft, misrepresentation, or exploitation.

3. Digital Addiction

With the immersive and engaging nature of VR, the risk of digital addiction could increase. As with other forms of digital media, overuse of VR could lead to negative health outcomes, including physical health issues such as sedentariness, and mental health issues like anxiety, depression, and sleep disorders.

Best Practices

Addressing these concerns requires a multi-faceted approach, involving VR developers, users, policy-makers, and mental health professionals. The following best practices aim to mitigate the potential adverse effects while enhancing the beneficial aspects of VR.

1. *Promoting Digital Literacy*

Digital literacy, including understanding the nuances of VR environments, should be promoted. Users should be educated about the potential risks associated with VR, such as derealization, depersonalization, and privacy concerns. They should be provided with tools and resources to manage their time in VR, protecting themselves against potential exploitation and digital addiction.

2. *Mindful Design Practices*

VR developers have a significant role to play in maintaining users' digital wellbeing. This can be achieved by incorporating mindful design practices, such as providing clear distinctions between VR and actual reality, implementing features that encourage breaks and promote healthy usage habits, and prioritizing user privacy and consent in the design and function of VR experiences.

3. *Robust Policy and Regulations*

Regulations must keep pace with technological advancements. Policies should be put in place to protect user data, to prevent exploitation, and to manage content within VR environments. These policies should be transparent, easy to understand, and firmly enforced.

4. *Mental Health Resources*

Given the potential psychological effects of VR, resources for mental health support should be readily available to users. This includes direct access to professional help, self-help resources, and community support within VR environments. Incorporating a mental health support system within the VR ecosystem can help address issues promptly, reducing the potential for harm.

As we embrace the transformative potential of virtual reality and the holographic mind theory, it is crucial to prioritize digital wellbeing in these new virtual spaces. By acknowledging the ethical concerns and adopting proactive measures, we can ensure that our journey into these novel realities is guided by the principles of respect, empathy, and care for individual and collective wellbeing.

Brain Privacy in the Age of Neurotechnology: A New Frontier for Human Rights

As we journey further into the age of neurotechnology, the fusion of neuroscience and virtual reality creates a new frontier for human rights, bringing forth the vital issue of "brain privacy." The notion of brain privacy is a new concept, stemming from advancements in neurotechnologies that can decode and influence brain activity. Today, it is not only a matter of understanding and protecting the privacy of our conscious thoughts but also our unconscious processes and intrinsic mental states.

The Neurotechnology Revolution

Over the past decade, neurotechnologies have made significant strides in mapping, decoding, and manipulating the brain's activity. These innovations range from non-invasive methods like EEG (electroencephalography) and fMRI (functional magnetic resonance imaging) to invasive technologies like deep brain stimulation and neural implants.

These technologies, designed to help us better understand the brain, treat neurological disorders, and enhance human capabilities, also pose novel ethical challenges. For instance, what happens when these technologies fall into the wrong hands? Could they be used to extract or manipulate a person's thoughts, emotions, or memories without consent? These questions bring us to the forefront of the ethical debate about brain privacy.

Brain Privacy: A New Human Right

The concept of brain privacy can be understood as the right to keep one's neural data private. It encompasses the protection of the content of our thoughts and experiences, our emotions, our decision-making processes, and any other cognitive or affective processes that can be inferred from brain data.

However, unlike personal data shared online, which can often be altered or deleted, neural data is intrinsically linked to an individual and cannot be changed. This characteristic makes neural data particularly sensitive and potentially damaging if misused.

Ethical Challenges and Concerns

The advent of neurotechnology opens up several ethical challenges and concerns:

1. Involuntary Mind Reading

As neurotechnologies advance, we inch closer to the possibility of decoding an individual's thoughts and emotions without their knowledge or consent. In the wrong hands, these technologies could lead to what is essentially mind reading, infringing on individuals' rights to mental privacy.

2. Manipulation and Control

Neurotechnologies that can influence brain activity present another significant ethical concern. These technologies, designed for therapeutic purposes like treating depression or Parkinson's disease, could potentially be misused for manipulation or control.

3. Neurodata Theft and Misuse

As with any form of data, neural data could potentially be stolen and misused. The implications of such a scenario are vast and unsettling, including identity theft, discrimination, and even the falsification of neural data.

Safeguarding Brain Privacy

Safeguarding brain privacy in the age of neurotechnology requires a multi-faceted approach:

1. Legal Protections

A comprehensive legal framework is needed to protect brain privacy. Laws should clearly outline the rights of individuals concerning their neural data, addressing issues of consent, misuse of neurotechnology, and data protection.

2. Neuroethical Guidelines

Developers and users of neurotechnology should adhere to neuroethical guidelines, emphasizing respect for individuals' mental privacy and autonomy. These guidelines should be developed in collaboration with ethicists, scientists, policy-makers, and the public.

3. Public Awareness and Education

Given the complexity and novelty of these issues, raising public awareness and understanding is crucial. Individuals should be aware of their rights concerning their neural data and the potential risks and benefits of neurotechnology.

As we stand at the frontier of the age of neurotechnology, the safeguarding of brain privacy emerges as a fundamental issue. It requires not only our attention but our concerted effort and collaboration. It is a new frontier in human rights that we must navigate with care, ensuring that our mental lives' privacy and integrity are respected and protected.

The Potential of Neurotechnology: Opportunities and Threats

The potential of neurotechnology is vast and goes beyond the realm of medicine. These technologies can provide insights into human cognition, enable direct brain-to-computer communication, enhance human capabilities, and even offer the tantalizing possibility of merging the human mind with artificial intelligence. This confluence of opportunities and risks underscores the need for robust ethical standards and regulations.

1. Enhanced Human Abilities

Neurotechnology holds the potential for augmenting human capabilities - enhancing memory, boosting cognitive abilities, and even allowing us to communicate with machines using thought alone. However, this also brings up ethical issues related to access, fairness, and the potential for creating a neurotechnological divide between those who can afford such enhancements and those who cannot.

2. Brain-Computer Interfaces

With the advent of brain-computer interfaces (BCIs), we're seeing a revolution in the way humans interact with technology. BCIs have the potential to help those with paralysis or limb loss regain control of their bodies. But they also carry risks - could such devices be hacked, or could they be used without the user's knowledge or consent to gather neural data?

Creating a Future of Neurotechnology That Respects Human Rights

Our journey into the age of neurotechnology must be guided by ethical principles that respect and protect human rights. Here are a few suggestions:

1. Incorporate Ethics Early and Often

Ethical considerations should be an integral part of neurotechnology development, not an afterthought. Neuroethicists should be included in the development process from the outset, helping to identify potential issues and devise strategies to address them.

2. Establish Strong Governance

Strong governance frameworks are essential to ensure that neurotechnologies are used responsibly. This includes clear regulations on the use of neural data, safeguards to protect individual privacy, and mechanisms to ensure accountability.

3. Foster an Open Dialogue

An open dialogue between scientists, ethicists, policymakers, and the public is vital. This dialogue can help build a shared understanding of the benefits and risks of neurotechnology, foster public trust, and ensure that the development of these technologies is guided by societal values and needs.

We must remember that our primary goal is to enhance the human experience, not diminish it. Let us strive to create a future of neurotechnology that respects our human rights, values our privacy, and above all, upholds our shared human dignity.

Conclusion

Embracing the Uncertain: Charting the Future of the Holographic Mind and VR

As we draw this exploration of the holographic mind and virtual reality to a close, let's pause to appreciate the breathtaking vistas we've traversed, while acknowledging the uncharted territories still awaiting us. We've navigated through quantum physics, delved into neuroscience, immersed ourselves in the virtual reality revolution, and grappled with ethical implications of this intriguing intersection. The trek has been thrilling, insightful, and occasionally unnerving. It has stretched our minds and challenged our preconceptions about reality, consciousness, and what it means to be human.

Yet, for all we've uncovered, our journey is far from over. The holographic mind and virtual reality are frontier territories, laden with vast, unexplored expanses. The emergent nature of both fields ensures that the exciting discoveries of today will be the building blocks of tomorrow's revolutions. The amalgamation of these two worlds could reshape how we understand the mind, consciousness, and reality itself.

Unanswered Questions and Future Directions

The intersection of holographic mind theory and VR still presents a myriad of unresolved questions. Are our brains truly holographic in nature? Can virtual reality ever simulate our mental processes accurately? Can neurotechnology advance to the point where our brain patterns can be converted into a holographic VR experience, offering an inside look into our mental states?

The future directions of these disciplines are equally stimulating. Can we develop empathetic AI systems in VR environments that could revolutionize mental health treatment? Will ethical safeguards keep pace with the rapid advancements in neurotechnology to protect our mental privacy?

Indeed, the challenges we face are as profound as the opportunities that lie before us. The path to unlocking the secrets of the holographic mind and realizing the full potential of virtual reality is laden with technological, ethical, and societal hurdles. Yet, it's through facing these challenges that we will push the boundaries of knowledge, innovate, and drive progress.

As we move forward, it's crucial to ensure that these developments are anchored in ethical considerations and societal values. The goal isn't merely technological advancement, but the betterment of humanity. Advancements in VR and understanding of the holographic mind should be used to enhance our understanding of ourselves, enrich our experiences, and create more empathetic, inclusive societies.

In this exciting era of exploration and discovery, we must remember to stay curious, remain open-minded, and embrace the uncertainty. After all, it's in the depths of the unknown that the greatest discoveries are made. As we continue to navigate this fascinating intersection of the holographic mind and virtual reality, we may not only change how we perceive reality and consciousness but also, potentially, redefine what it means to be human in a technologically advanced world.

On this exhilarating journey of discovery, let's remember to cherish the mystery, marvel at the complexity of the human mind, and celebrate the power of technology to transform our understanding and experience of reality. The quest for knowledge is a journey, not a destination. As we chart the future of the holographic mind and virtual reality, we are, in fact, mapping out a vital part of our journey as a species – one that's full of potential and brimming with possibilities.

Empowering Humanity: The Potential of a Holographic Understanding

Embracing a holographic understanding of the mind can catalyze a seismic shift in how we view ourselves, our relationships, our societies, and our place in the universe. This paradigm, which casts consciousness as a hologram, has profound implications for multiple disciplines, including neuroscience, psychology, philosophy, and even the nascent field of virtual reality. Let's explore the immense potential that a holographic understanding of the mind could unlock for humanity.

Imagine a world where mental health professionals could view a patient's mind as a hologram, visualizing the interplay of thoughts, emotions, and memories. Such a perspective could revolutionize the diagnosis and treatment of mental health disorders, helping professionals identify problematic patterns, provide personalized interventions, and track treatment progress in unprecedented detail.

Imagine educators using holographic mind theory to shape learning experiences that cater to each student's unique cognitive style. By treating the mind as a hologram, they could create dynamic, adaptable educational strategies that promote deep understanding and foster a lifelong love of learning.

The implications extend beyond the practical. A holographic understanding of the mind could alter our philosophical and spiritual perspectives. If our minds are holographic, then each part of our consciousness contains the whole, suggesting an inherent interconnectedness and unity in our existence. This realization could cultivate empathy, compassion, and a sense of interconnectedness, empowering us to build more inclusive and understanding societies.

A holographic understanding also offers fertile ground for interdisciplinary innovation. Consider the field of artificial intelligence. If our minds are holographic, might we build artificial intelligences that reflect this structure? AI with a holographic structure could possess an unprecedented degree of adaptability and creativity, opening new horizons in technology and society.

At the crossroads of holographic mind theory and digital technology lies the exciting realm of virtual reality. By modeling our mental processes in VR, we could explore the architecture of our minds in new ways. Imagine VR applications that allow us to interact with our thoughts, emotions, and memories in a visual and tactile manner, providing us with invaluable insights into our cognitive patterns and emotional dynamics.

Moreover, as VR technology advances, we could potentially simulate holographic minds, allowing us to experience different mental states and perspectives. This could foster empathy by enabling us to see the world through another's eyes, or provide novel therapeutic tools by allowing us to navigate and reshape our mental landscapes.

Yet, the journey toward fully realizing the potential of a holographic understanding is not without challenges. As with any paradigm shift, it necessitates a willingness to question long-standing assumptions and navigate the unknown. Moreover, as we venture into the uncharted territories of the mind and VR, we must grapple with ethical dilemmas, from the privacy of our thoughts to the potential impacts of radically new experiences on our psyche.

Notably, the path forward must be paved with an unwavering commitment to harnessing the holographic understanding for the benefit of all. The goal is not merely to advance our knowledge or to develop new technologies, but to empower humanity. By enhancing our self-understanding, enriching our experiences, and fostering empathy and compassion, a holographic understanding could catalyze our growth as individuals and as a society.

A holographic understanding of the mind harbors immense potential, presenting opportunities for breakthroughs in diverse fields, from neuroscience and education to artificial intelligence and virtual reality. It invites us to reimagine our self-conception, our relationships, and our societies. It beckons us to chart a path of exploration that is guided by curiosity, driven by the pursuit of knowledge, and imbued with a commitment to fostering well-being and understanding. As we embark on this journey, let's embrace the potential of a holographic understanding to empower us, to bring us closer together, and to illuminate the richness of the human experience.

The holographic theory of the mind serves as a powerful reminder of the intricacies of our consciousness and how each piece, each thought, and every fragment of a memory can play a role in forming our complete cognitive picture.

By harnessing this perspective, we might better understand the complexities of mental disorders, cognitive development, and even aspects of consciousness that have long eluded us.

It also has vast implications for our understanding of collective consciousness. If each part of our minds contains the entirety of our cognitive experiences, then the combination of these experiences across all humans has the potential to form a vast, interconnected network of shared knowledge, ideas, and perspectives. This realization could be a catalyst for the development of more collaborative and empathetic societies, moving us away from a paradigm of individualism and competition towards one of interconnectedness and collective growth.

In the world of artificial intelligence, this understanding could provide us with new strategies for developing more advanced, adaptable, and human-like AI systems. By incorporating holographic principles into AI design, we could create machines capable of learning and problem-solving in ways that more closely mirror human cognition. This could potentially lead to advancements in AI technology that we are only just beginning to imagine.

Yet, as we delve deeper into this understanding and explore its potential applications, we must also confront critical ethical questions. How do we ensure the privacy and security of our inner thoughts in a world where technology is increasingly intertwined with our minds?

How do we navigate the potential psychological impacts of experiencing alternative realities or radically different mental states?

These questions underscore the importance of approaching this new frontier with caution, ensuring that our exploration of the holographic mind and its applications in VR and AI are guided by a commitment to ethics, respect for individual autonomy, and an understanding of the potential psychological implications.

As we chart the course for the future of the holographic mind and VR, we must embrace the uncertainty that comes with venturing into uncharted territory. There will be unanswered questions and challenges along the way, but these unknowns should not deter us. Instead, they should fuel our curiosity and motivate us to explore, learn, and grow. By approaching this journey with an open mind and a commitment to ethical exploration, we can navigate the challenges and uncertainties that lie ahead.

In the end, the exploration of the holographic mind and its intersection with VR presents an exciting journey into the depths of human consciousness. It offers a new lens through which we can view the mind, and by extension, our reality. By exploring and embracing the potential of this understanding, we can unlock new possibilities for individual growth, societal advancement, and a deeper understanding of what it means to be human.

The holographic understanding of the mind, as complex and elusive as it may be, holds a mirror to the infinite potential of human consciousness. It is an invitation to question, explore, and marvel at the intricate tapestry of our minds.

Final Thoughts

As we close the curtain on this exploration of the intersection of neuroscience and virtual reality, guided by the holographic theory of the mind, it is fitting to pause and reflect on the journey we have embarked on. It has been a path that has invited us to question the very nature of consciousness, cognition, and the human experience, one that has brought us to the forefront of technological innovation and human understanding.

At the core of this journey lies the holographic mind - a concept as fascinating as it is complex. It challenges us to reimagine our understanding of cognition and consciousness, to envision a brain that operates not merely on the principles of linear connectivity but as a vast, intricate, and interconnected network where each part contains a representation of the whole. It is a perspective that draws inspiration from the principles of quantum physics and holography, bridging seemingly disparate fields in a unifying vision of the human mind.

The holographic mind not only challenges our understanding of the brain and consciousness but also provides a powerful metaphor for understanding human nature and our connection with the world. Just as every piece of a hologram contains the information of the whole, each individual carries within them a reflection of the collective human experience. This understanding underscores our interconnectedness and interdependence, inviting us to cultivate empathy, compassion, and collective responsibility.

The journey then takes us into the realm of virtual reality - a technology that has the power to augment our perception and redefine our experience of reality. Here we see the potential of VR as a tool to explore, simulate, and potentially even enhance our mental processes. We also begin to see how VR could serve as a practical tool to investigate the holographic mind theory, enabling us to create immersive cognitive experiences and observe their impact on our neural networks.

As we venture into the world of artificial intelligence, we are confronted with the possibilities and challenges of translating the holographic mind into a computational model. The intersection of neuroscience and AI is a rich field of exploration, one that holds the potential to revolutionize our understanding of both human and artificial cognition. It invites us to contemplate the prospects of empathetic AI, neurofeedback systems, and even the potential for an AI that operates on principles similar to the holographic mind.

Yet, with these exciting possibilities comes a new ethical frontier. Our journey brings us face-to-face with critical questions about privacy, autonomy, and psychological well-being in the age of neurotechnology and virtual realities. As we delve deeper into the understanding of the holographic mind and its intersection with VR and AI, we must ensure that our explorations are guided by ethical considerations, a respect for individual rights, and a thorough understanding of potential psychological implications.

As we approach the end of our journey, we stand on the cusp of a new understanding of the mind and reality. A future where the boundaries between the physical and virtual, the individual and the collective, the tangible and the intangible continue to blur. It's a future that holds great promise, but also great responsibility.

In this future, the holographic mind is not just a theory of cognition, but a framework for understanding our interconnectedness and our collective responsibility to each other and to our shared reality. It is a reminder that, just as every part of a hologram contains the whole, every individual action and decision contributes to the collective outcome.

Finally, as we chart the course forward, it's crucial to remember that the exploration of the holographic mind and its intersection with virtual reality is a journey of discovery and learning. As we continue to explore, investigate, and push the boundaries of our understanding, we will undoubtedly encounter new questions, challenges, and surprises along the way. And in the face of these unknowns, let's embrace the spirit of curiosity and exploration that has guided us on this journey.

This exploration of the holographic mind, the intersections of neuroscience and virtual reality, the ethical implications and the technological developments, is not only an academic or technological pursuit, but it's also deeply personal. It informs the way we perceive ourselves, the world, and our place within it. It shapes our understanding of cognition, consciousness, empathy, and even identity.

With the expansion of VR technologies, we are presented with new tools to explore our minds, emotions, and cognitive processes. We are given a new lens to perceive and experience realities beyond our physical boundaries. But it's critical to ensure that these technologies, as they continue to evolve and permeate our lives, are developed and used responsibly and ethically.

Consider the implications of a world where your mind's deepest secrets could potentially be accessed, or a scenario where thoughts and emotions could be manipulated. These are not merely hypotheticals. As technology continues to advance, these could become real ethical dilemmas that we must navigate.

We must also consider the broader societal implications. As we enhance our mental capacities or immerse ourselves in virtual realities, we must question how these advancements will impact our social structures, our relationships, and our understanding of what it means to be human. In other words, the emergence of these technologies should be accompanied by thoughtful and inclusive discussions about their potential societal impacts.

As we move forward, one thing is certain: we are entering an era of uncharted territory. The intersection of the holographic mind theory and virtual reality has opened up a world of possibilities that were unimaginable just a few decades ago. As we stand on the brink of this new era, it's crucial that we approach it with a spirit of curiosity, responsibility, and respect for the profound implications of our discoveries.

As we conclude, it's important to remember that this journey is far from over. We have only just begun to scratch the surface of the holographic mind theory and its intersection with virtual reality. There is still much to discover, to learn, and to understand. This journey is a testament to our relentless pursuit of knowledge, our capacity for innovation, and our innate curiosity about the inner workings of our minds.

Embrace the journey, embrace the uncertainty, and look forward to the future with a sense of hope and excitement. The exploration of the holographic mind and its intersections with virtual reality is a testament to our collective ingenuity, resilience, and aspiration for a deeper understanding of ourselves and the world around us.

As we continue to delve deeper into this realm of endless possibilities, we'll no doubt encounter challenges, make mistakes, and face ethical dilemmas. Yet, it's through these trials and errors that we learn, grow, and make strides toward progress. We are on the cusp of a new era, one in which our understanding of the mind, reality, and human nature will be transformed forever. It's a future that's filled with promise, excitement, and a wealth of unexplored territories.

In the end, the holographic mind theory and the world of virtual reality invite us to consider not just how we perceive the world, but also how we understand ourselves. It's a call to continuously question, explore, and marvel at the mysteries of the mind and the universe. So, let's venture forward into this brave new world, with open minds, compassionate hearts, and a relentless drive for discovery.

Let's continue the journey, for it promises to be an incredible one.

Stay safe, stay well, and always remain curious.

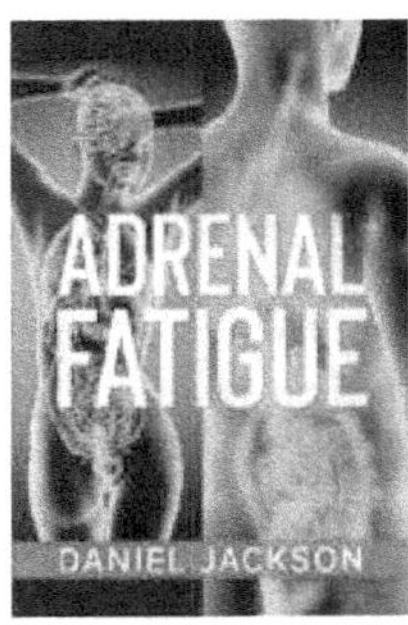

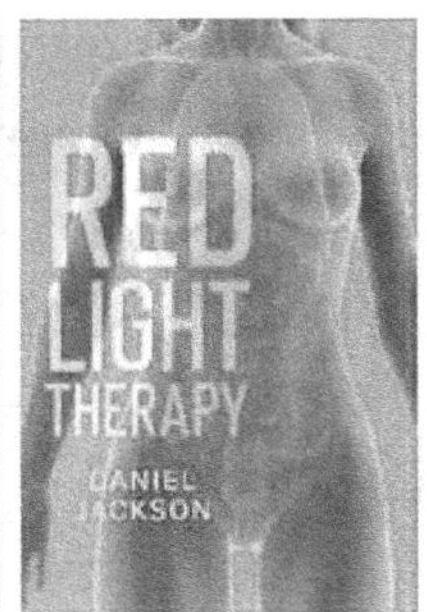

Take a look at more great books available from Rockwood Publishing

... some for FREE!

Just visit the link below:

rockwoodpublishing.co.uk

websites listed in this book. The inclusion of any website links does not necessarily imply a recommendation or endorse the views expressed within them. Rockwood Publishing takes no responsibility for, and will not be liable for, the websites being temporarily unavailable or being removed from the Internet. The accuracy and completeness of information provided herein and opinions stated herein are not guaranteed or warranted to produce any particular results, and the advice and strategies contained herein may not be suitable for every individual. The author shall not be liable for any loss incurred as a consequence of the use and application, directly or indirectly, of any information presented in this work. This publication is designed to provide information in regards to the subject matter covered. The information included in this book has been compiled to give an overview of the subject(s) and detail some of the symptoms, treatments etc. that are available to people with this condition. It is not intended to give medical advice. For a firm diagnosis of your condition, and for a treatment plan suitable for you, you should consult your doctor or consultant. The writer of this book and the publisher are not responsible for any damages or negative consequences following any of the treatments or methods highlighted in this book. Website links are for informational purposes and should not be seen as a personal endorsement; the same applies to the products detailed in this book. The reader should also be aware that although the web links included were correct at the time of writing, they may become out of date in the future.

Disclaimers

The content contained within this book is for information and entertainment purposes only, and in no way purports to represent professional medical opinion. It should NOT be used as a substitute for expert advice, and you must consult with your designated health professional before acting upon any information contained herein or before undertaking any practice whose methodology is referred to in this book. The author is NOT a registered health professional and the text merely represents personal opinion, not medical fact. The author cannot be held responsible for the consequences of any action derived from the reading of this book, as the content is not based on diagnosis and subsequent regimen. It is the reader's responsibility to seek proper, professional medical advice from a registered health practitioner in connection with any material contained within this book.

Legal Disclaimer (part 1)

Nothing in this book should be construed as an attempt to diagnose, treat or cure. The information in this book is intended to be a community resource. The author takes no responsibility for any informational material or brochures produced using information taken from this book. The author has endeavoured to ensure that all information is correct at the time of publication. This information, however, is subject to change without notice. The author makes no warranty with regard to the accuracy of any information and will not be liable for any errors or omissions. Any liability that arises as a result of this information is hereby excluded to the fullest extent allowed by law.

This information should not be used as a substitute for seeking independent professional advice.

Legal Disclaimer (part 2)

Disclaimer and Terms of Use:

a) i. In publishing this information, the author makes no representations concerning the efficacy, appropriateness or suitability of any products or treatments. Use this information at your own risk. The compiler is not a doctor and has no medical background or training.

ii. Statements and information regarding dietary supplements, books and any products mentioned have not been evaluated by any health authority and are not intended to diagnose, treat, cure or prevent any disease or health condition.

b) In view of the possibility of human error, neither the author nor any other party involved in providing this information, warrant that the information contained therein is in every respect accurate or complete and they are not responsible nor liable for any errors or omissions that may be found or for the results obtained from the use of such information. The entire risk as to use of this information is assumed by the user.

c) You are encouraged to consult other sources and confirm the information.

d) The information you access is provided "as is". No warranty, expressed or implied, is given as to the accuracy, completeness or timeliness of any information herein, or for obtaining legal advice. To the fullest extent permissible pursuant to applicable law, neither the author nor any other parties who have been involved in the creation, preparation, printing, or delivering of this information assume responsibility for the completeness, accuracy, timeliness, errors or omissions of said information and assume no liability for any direct, incidental, consequential, indirect, or punitive damages as well as any circumstance for any complication, injuries, side effects or other medical accidents to person or property arising from or in connection with the use or reliance upon any information contained herein.

e) The author is not responsible for the contents of any linked site or any link contained in a linked site, or any changes or update to such sites. The inclusion of any link does not imply endorsement by the author. The author makes no representations or claims as to the quality, content and accuracy of the information, services, products, messages which may be provided by such resources, and specifically disclaims any warranties, including but not limited to implied or express warranties of merchantability or fitness for any particular usage, application or purpose.

f) The information provided is general in nature and is intended for educational and informational purposes only. It is not intended to replace or substitute the evaluation, judgment, diagnosis, and medical or preventative care of a physician, paediatrician, therapist and/or health care provider.

g) Any medical, nutritional, dietetic, therapeutic or other decisions, dosages, treatments or drug regimes should be made in consultation with a health care practitioner. Do not discontinue treatment or medication without first consulting your physician, clinician or therapist.

h) By reading this information, you signify your assent to these terms and conditions of use. If you do not agree to these terms and conditions of use, do not read/use this information. If any provision of these terms and conditions of use shall be determined to be unlawful, void or for any reason unenforceable, then that provision shall be deemed severable from this agreement and shall not affect the validity and enforceability of any remaining provisions.

i) The information, services, products, messages and other materials, individually and collectively, are provided with the understanding that the author is not engaged in rendering medical advice or recommendations.

j) The information and the terms of use are subject to change without notice. The material provided as is without warranty of any kind and may include inaccuracies and/or typographical errors. The author makes no representations about the suitability of this information for any purpose. The author disclaims all warranties with regard to this information, including all implied warranties, and in no event shall the author be held liable, resulting from, or in any way related to, the use of this information.

k) The unauthorized alteration of the content of this information is expressly prohibited. The author, its agents and representatives shall not be responsible for any claims, actions or damages which may arise on account of the unauthorized alteration of this information.

www.ingramcontent.com/pod-product-compliance
Lightning Source LLC
Chambersburg PA
CBHW071317130726
47996CB00002B/521